Sacred Conspiracy

A Commentary to the Fukushima Ryu Shinobi-no-Maki

By

Steven Nojiri

Profound Dedication

Any and all merit generated from this book is dedicated to the enlightenment of all sentient beings.

Any and all virtue stemming from this project is dedicated to the Buddha, the Dharma, and the Sangha.

Dedication

This book is dedicated to the all the men and women involved in the history contained within this book.

In particular, this book is dedicated to the history and future prosperity of the House of Nojiri.

Deep Thanks

To my guru, who put me on the path and continues to guide me.

To my wife, who continues to love and support me.

To the House of Nojiri, for allowing me the honor of duty and obligation

Acknowledgements

To the House of Nojiri, my family, who provided me with a multitude of manuals, tradition, and history.

To Antony Cummins and his team, for providing me with a full copy of Fujita Seiko's copy of the root text and the annotations.

Introduction

Allow me to begin by stating that I am very humbled and honored to have this opportunity to present this Fukushima Ryu commentary to the general public. I have always had a deep respect for Fukushima Ryu and the history surrounding the system. However, I was unable to go into great detail regarding the system because I only possessed hearsay and fragments of the manuals belonging to the tradition.

However, through my association with ninjutsu researcher Antony Cummins and his work, I was given a copy Fujita Seiko's transcription of the root text with the accompanying annotations (written ~200 years after the main text). Originally, I had informed Antony Cummins of the manual and its connection to my family's history. Antony Cummins promised me that, if he ever obtained a copy of the manual, he would pass it on to me. Antony almost found the manual on a few occasions, but years passed with no results. Antony and I eventually parted ways due to ideological differences in 2012.

However, in 2013, a series of auspicious events lined up and Antony obtained a full copy of Fujita Seiko's transcription of the root text and annotations. More importantly, Antony kept his word. He contacted me and gave me a copy of the text. Immediately I sat down and went through the text, kanji by kanji, comparing its contents to the oral tradition and fragments in my possession. I was elated.

Antony and his team have gone on to translate and publish the manual in their own works, and I wish them success in their efforts.

This book, however, is my commentary on the manual. Antony Cummins provided his team's translation, to which I am thankful. However, I have gone through the text and translated many of the sections as I see fit. My translations, therefore, will not match Antony's team's work. I think this is very good for the readers, as the readers will be allowed two different translations from which to glean the actual meaning.

I also take this moment to remind the reader that this text, while small and simple, was also very hard to read grammatically. Some segments have multiple ways to be interpreted, with each interpretation fitting the context and making sense. As such, many parts of the translation are an amalgamation of the different meanings. I have chosen to go with this approach in order to try and capture the full spectrum of meaning behind the line of text. In some places, I paraphrase or change the wording so that it makes sense in English. This is to avoid confusion and potential erroneous assumptions. There are a few lines of text which could easily be greatly misinterpreted if translated literally, leading to all manner of erroneous thinking and mistaken ideas regarding the content.

Warning to the Reader

I should also warn the reader that my commentary is based on my own personal understanding of history and tradition. I make no promises as to historical accuracy of anything I say. This book is not meant to be a history book. Rather, this book is meant to be one Nojiri family member's thoughts on the matter. Nothing more. Nothing less.

With that said, I wish to move forward into some background history which is vital to understanding Fukushima Ryu ninjutsu.

Also, I would like the reader to understand the value of this Fukushima Ryu manual outside of its role as a shinobi manual. Far deeper than being just one more ninja document in the historical record, the manual also serves as a historical marker - a brief glimpse- into the larger and deeper political, cultural, and spiritual narratives of the individuals involved in formation of Fukushima Ryu.

Table of Contents

Chapter 1: Background Information
Go-Daigo's Intention and the Southern Court
Kusunoki Ryu
The "Servant, the "House", and the "Son of Heaven"
The Origin of Shinobi-no-Jutsu

Chapter 2: Preliminary Details
The Origin of Fukushima Ryu
Inko Ryu
Serving as Chief Retainers
Fukushima Ryu is not Iga Ryu
The Magic
Fukushima Ryu Shinobi-no-Maki
Author's Interruption

Chapter 3: Fukushima Ryu Shinobi-no-Maki Commentary

Chapter 4: Addendum – Brief Survey of Kusunoki Ryu

Chapter 5: Conclusion
Espionage and Magic: Two Distinct Aspects
Follow-up: The House of Fukushima
Follow-up: The House of Nojiri/Kumazawa
Follow-up: The Southern Court Loyalists
Follow-up: Fukushima Ryu
Final Comments

CHAPTER 1

Background Information

Go-Daigo's Intention and the Southern Court

The readers of my previous work, IN PRAISE OF SPIES (2012), were introduced to a piece of Japanese political and cultural history known as the Go-Nancho, the Second Southern Court. This is a topic rarely addressed by Japanese scholars and, rarer still, in any English document. I discuss it now because it provides a critical context for the history surrounding the manual.

As the topic of the Nanbokucho period, the war between the first Southern Court and the Northern Court, is greatly documented, this book will not rehash this material to a great extent.

Simply put, Go-Daigo Tenno wanted to pull the control of the country away from the House of Hojo and restore government that was run by civil administration, not martial law. The House of Hojo put up a massive resistance and a countrywide war took place. Readers should also be aware that it was during this period that Kusunoki Masashige committed all of his legendary actions and formed his espionage tradition. Go-Daigo's forces won and the Kemmu Restoration took place.

However, one of Go-Daigo's generals, named Ashikaga Takauji, betrayed Go-Daigo and sieged Kyoto. Ashikaga demanded the title of shogun. Go-Daigo refused. War erupted. Ashikaga established an alternate and illegitimate imperial line, which operated out of Kyoto. Go-Daigo, the real Emperor, operated out of Yoshino. The illegitimate court was labeled the Northern Court and Go-Daigo's legitimate court was labeled the Southern Court. This lasted until the 1390s, when a peace treaty was reached between the two courts. However, the Northern Court broke this treaty soon after.

All of this history is standard and easily researchable. It is what happened next that is considered a taboo topic, even today. Simply put, historians and scholars will tell you that the Northern Court's betrayal went unchallenged and the Southern Court faded away.

This is false.

The Southern Court reorganized after the treaty was broken and formed the Go-Nancho, the "Second Southern Court". This court began a constant resistance, both of ideology and military campaigns, against the Northern Court Pretenders from the late 1300s until this very day. During the 1400s, the Go-Nancho was behind the assassination of an Ashikaga Shogun. The conflict between Hosokawa and Yamana, which incited the Onin War, has roots in the Go-Nancho's campaign. It was also during this time period that, according to Go-Nancho tradition, the Loyalists stole the three articles of Imperial Regalia. While the Northern Court managed to retrieve two of the items, one item of the regalia was not retrieved. It was replaced with a fake. While the replacing of an item is known to some historians, the identity of which item that was replaced is still considered something to only be passed down by word of mouth. As such, I will respect this and not publish the identity of the item.

Also, Southern Court Loyalists filled Oda Nobunaga's forces, leading some to wonder if Nobunaga's decision to ignore the illegitimate Emperor and to ultimately crush the Ashikaga Shogunate wasn't somehow influenced by the Go-Nancho Loyalists.

One of the major military systems associated with the Go-Nancho Loyalists was the Kusunoki Ryu, whose main root texts are, collectively, referred to as the *Taiheiki Hidensho* (The document of the Secret Tradition of The Great Peace). This is an alternate Taiheiki, written not from the Ashikaga perspective, but from the Go-Nancho perspective. We will examine this collective of documents near the end of this book. While many non-Southern Court families and clans eventually ended up with Kusunoki Ryu teachings, the Southern Court Loyalists specifically maintained study of this material. The main line of Kusunoki Ryu was also found among Oda Nobunaga's retainers. The head of the main line, Kusunoki Masatora, served Oda Nobunaga in the late 1500s.

During the Edo period, the head of the Kusunoki Ryu Gungaku organization, a man named Yui Shosetsu, led the Keian revolt in an attempt to topple the Tokugawa Shogunate. Even though the revolt failed, it did manage to change the laws and legal policies regarding samurai hiring and job security.

Southern Court Loyalists still maintain this resistance even at present. This resistance was recorded by major news outlets in Japan during the early 1900s, when a man by the name of Kumazawa Taizen began discussions with Emperor Meiji about abdicating the throne to Taizen. Meiji never abdicated the throne, but he did openly support Kumazawa, even issuing Kumazawa a letter admitting that Kumazawa was the real Emperor. This was a huge gesture, considering this was the same time period where individuals could be, and were, executed for any efforts made against the illegitimate court. For example, a man by the name of Shushui Kotoku was executed in the early 1900s for publically shouting out (to members of the illegitimate court) a comment along the lines of *"Isn't this court fraudulent? Is it not the fake Northern Court which betrayed the real Southern Court?"* It should also be noted by the reader that many other Southern Court Loyalists and supporters were killed during the period of 1868-1945.

Taizen's son, Hiromichi, made an effort to regain control. Hiromichi even met with American HQ after World War 2 in an attempt to gain support. He did not get it. He then traveled the country, attempting to rally support. However, the illegitimate Imperial House of the time began to make is life very hard. Several of Hiromichi's retainers we attacked and jailed on false charges. Some were forced to flee the country. Hiromichi's son, Takanobu, had been imprisoned in Siberia (due to participating in military operations on the Chinese/Russian border). Upon return, he was docile in his stance for a long time due to his time in the prison camp. In fact, for many years, he was opposed to supporting any imperial system. Later in life, he realized his ignorance. Out of filial devotion and sense of duty and obligation to the tradition, he also led a small push towards a Go-Nancho Restoration. However, his efforts earned him, his family, and his supporters a rather nasty response from the illegitimate court.

And thus, we arrive at the reason why I have mentioned all of the above, regarding the Go-Nancho and Kusunoki Ryu. Simply put, the reader needs to understand the framework of these two entities before going directly into the origin of the Fukushima Ryu. The Fukushima Ryu was created by individuals who were born, raised, trained, and steeped in the traditions of Go-Nancho and various branches of Kusunoki Ryu. Having a clear understanding of this prolonged campaign of the Southern Court gives insight into the world of the men who created the system and the overall context.

Kusunoki Ryu

As stated, Kusunoki Ryu was a system based on the military tactics which were formed by Kusunoki Masashige during the wars of the Kemmu Restoration. Kusunoki Masashige got the majority of his tactics from the *Six Secret Teachings, Sun Tzu Tactics*, and pre-existing Genji (Minamoto) tactics. These tactics were passed down to Masashige's two sons, Masatsura and Masanori. Masatsura died young and Masanori survived into old age. The main line of Kusunoki Ryu is better known as Kusunoki Masanori Ryu, as Masanori reorganized and reworked his father's tactics. Thus, while Masashige is credited as the founder, the material that has passed down the mainline is actually more related to Masanori. Several branches and descendants of this system spread throughout Japan over the course of hundreds of years. Some of these branches were related to Go-Nancho efforts, many were not. The Fukushima Ryu is, in my opinion, a descendant of Kusunoki Ryu.

The "Servant, the "House", and the "Son of Heaven"

In order to better understand the socio-political, and I dare say, the cultural context of the world of the founder of Fukushima Ryu, we need to take a moment to properly understand the relationship between samurai, the House, and the Tenno.

Simply put, there are many academic writings which go into this relationship in extreme detail. This level of detail is beyond the scope of this book. For this book, I will only briefly survey this relationship so that the reader has a basic understanding.

Ideally, the Emperor, called Tenno ("Son of Heaven"), rules the country with divine right. Being a descendant of Amaterasu O-kami, the Sun Goddess, the Tenno is the representative of the Amaterasu O-kami's will and activities. The samurai that serve the Tenno, many of which are believed to descend from various gods themselves (as many samurai families claim descent from various Shinto deities), exist within a very specific relationship. The samurai, as an individual, is a piece of a larger entity: The House. "House", in this case, can also be translated as "Family" or "Clan". However, in keeping with the English language (with a history of European gentry traditions), I have chosen, as have many other historians, to use the word "House". Thus, rather than saying "Fukushima Clan", I will be saying "House of Fukushima". I feel that this will convey a more appropriate approximation to the historical reality.

In theory, the Tenno is served by all and every noble House, similar to the way European kings were lord over all European "Houses". Originally, there was a distinction between Court Noble Houses and Bushi Houses. The power structure was:

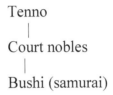

That is, the Court Nobles outranked the bushi, and as such, the bushi usually answered to the court nobles. However, spiritually speaking, the court nobles were conveying the wishes of the Tenno to the bushi. As such, the bushi were, at least in theory, serving the Emperor.

As time marched on, the samurai obtained more and more control over the government. The key event which cemented samurai control was the Genpei War. In this war, the House of Taira (Heishi) pushed for a massive military coupe of the government. The House of Genji (Minamoto) defended the Imperial Throne, but in the wake of the war, the House of Genji maintained political dominance in the form of a military-run government. This effectively negated the Court Nobles from the equation. Now, the country was run by the bushi. Still, even with this turn of events, the Tenno was spiritually the leader of the country and all service to the shogun and any bushi house was considered service to the Tenno. Since all the bushi houses answered to the Shogun, and the Shogun's authority stemmed from his appointment by the Tenno, the ideology continued to support the reality.

However, when the House of Hojo effectively pulled all real control away from the Imperial Throne, Emperor Go-Daigo launched the Kemmu Restoration to restore spiritual and political balance. Depending on how you view history, this balance was either restored or not restored.

Neutral bushi and bushi who sided with the Northern Court believed that serving the illegitimate northern emperor was service to the Tenno. For those samurai, their service to various daimyo and Houses during the Onin War and Sengoku Jidai follows the standard ideology that their existence as samurai is based on the trickle-down authority that comes from the Tenno.

Southern Court Loyalists consider that the only true service to the Tenno is service to the legitimate Southern Court Emperor. As such, there is a unique ideology at play in the Southern Court Loyalists, an ideology that allowed espionage and clandestine behavior to thrive within their tactics. For example, a Southern Court Loyalist had no issue with betraying one faction if it meant moving the pieces of the political chessboard into advantageous positions. For the Southern Court Loyalists, espionage and conspiracy was a sacred rite, an act of Shinto.

The ideals of Bushido that would form in the Edo period were not beheld by the Southern Court Loyalists. Service to a Lord, to the extent demanded by such codes and ideologies, were wasted on a system founded on military leaders serving a fake Emperor.

That is not to say that non-Southern Court families were blindly loyal and patriotic to their Lords either. Remember, we are discussing ideologies, not "forensic realities". The reality is that many samurai Houses, despite their alleged ideology, were really only looking out for the interests of their own House. Loyal service to Daimyo and Shoguns was, usually, not out of spiritual obligations, but rather, out of the need to secure one's own House.

Thus, despite ideologies and spiritual concepts, the reality is that most samurai placed their own House first and foremost. A samurai was nothing without his House, and consequently, a House was nothing without its loyal members. Thus, a typical samurai would have to balance the security and fame of his own House with any political ideologies he may or may not have.

In this way, we see that the House of Nojiri/Kumazawa had to not only maintain the Go-Nancho agenda, but they also had to push their own specific House into a position of power and security. It is for this reason that we see the House of Nojiri turn to the House of Oda in the mid-1500s.

The Origin of Shinobi-no-Jutsu

Shinobi-no-jutsu is large collection of various guerilla and espionage techniques. Pinpointing a single origin is as impossible as it is grossly misrepresentative of the dynamic of shinobi-no-jutsu's existence. In fact, the reality is that, more than likely, it has no single origin point. Realistically, it is the result of dozens of traditions mingling among the samurai Houses of feudal Japan. However, each of these traditions usually have an origin story. Thus, rather than trying to find the origin to ninjutsu itself, we should look at the origin of each system individually.

Fukushima Ryu's origin is simple: The House of Nojiri created it upon the request of Fukushima Masanori. (This will be discussed in the next section.)

However, is there an alleged origin for the shinobi arts among the traditions from which the House of Nojiri crafted the Fukushima Ryu? Is there an origin beyond the Kusunoki Ryu and Southern Court, as both claim to have gotten the material from previous sources? Kusunoki Masashige, and other Southern Court bushi, claimed to have gotten their material from Chinese writings and Genji tactics. The Chinese texts mentioned are, predominately, the *Six Secret Teachings* and the *Sun Tzu Tactics*. But, what about the Genji teachings?

I must warn the reader that what I am about to present is oral tradition and I have no way to prove or back this up. As such, enjoy the story and understand this is oral tradition without documentation.

With that disclaimer, I will present the oral tradition, which may or may not be real. Despite its probable creation hundreds of years after the alleged event, what is important is the symbolism and spiritual significance of the story.

The oral tradition simply states:

"The origin of ninjutsu is found the secret arts (hijutsu) passed to Genji Yorimitsu by Hachiman Daibosatsu. This was used, in the beginning, to rescue hostages and kill enemies defending secure locations. Later, it was adapted into ninjutsu. This is known as the Hachiman Daibosatsu Tradition."

Genji Yorimitsu was a Genji samurai who lived between 948-1021 a.d. He was a renowned warrior and the House of Nojiri (the Nojiri line) traces part of its genealogical descent from him. In fact, our most used family crest is a mitsudomoe because of this reason. Genji Yorimitsu started the Settsu branch of the House of Genji, and many powerful samurai Houses came from the Settsu branch.

It is believed that this specific event took place in 990, when Genji Yorimitsu was in his early 40s. This coincides with a very famous story involving Genji Yorimitsu. According to popular folklore, it was around this time that Yorimitsu and his retainers saved a group of women from a pack of malicious Oni in the mountains. This is known throughout Japan as the "Story of Shuten Doji". However, the oral tradition tells a different version of the story.

In the oral tradition, a great flood took place in 989. After this flood, many women around Kyoto were missing. Many presumed them to be killed in the flood. However, women kept disappearing, even after the flood had finished. Officials went to ask Abe no Seimei, a powerful Taoist sorcerer, to use his powers to learn the reason for the missing girls. Abe no Seimei divined that the women were being kidnapped and eaten by a group of cannibal bandits. However, due to several factors, Abe no Seimei could not divine the location of their base, just that the base was somewhere in the mountains outside of Kyoto. Genji Yorimitsu was called forth by the Emperor to locate the cannibals, kill them, and rescue the women.

It was at this point that Genji Yorimitsu and his retainers are said to have gone into local temples and shrines to conduct prayers and meditation. Genji Yorimitsu's prayers are the key focus of the tradition.

Genji Yorimitsu entered into deep prayer and meditation, asking for the help from Buddhas and Shinto Deities to save these women and put an end to the cannibals and their negative deeds (which cause suffering to society and future suffering, in the form of negative karma, for the cannibals themselves).

According to the oral tradition, Hachiman Daibosatsu (the Shinto God of Archery and Warfare who converted to Buddhism and has a connection to Amida Buddha) appeared to Genji Yorimitsu and taught him the secret arts, Hijutsu. This Hijutsu would, generations later, become the ninjutsu of this tradition. Hachiman Daibosatsu taught that warfare was unnatural to the world of men, that it had been given to man by Asuras (war mongering demi-gods) and that the Gods were giving man Hijutsu to preempt warfare. This was considered the beginning of *"dismantling the enemy's plans for war before the enemy can attack"*.

It is also said that the astrological gods of the Orion Belt constellation visited Genji Yorimitsu, regarding navigation. Yorimitsu is said to also have seen Avalokitesvara, Medicine Buddha, as well as the vision of Hachiman Daibosatsu ending in a vision of Amida Buddha.

Because of these three specific deities, some say that the shrine Yorimitsu prayed at was the Kumano Shrine, or if not the main shrine, one of the branch shrines. Alternate versions say he prayed specifically at a Hachiman Shrine and that there is no correlation. Other explanations say that it was a Hachiman Shrine, but that the vision projected from the Kumano Shrine. Interestingly enough, the Buddhist priest Ippen (1239-89), is reported to have had a vision of Amida Buddha at the Kumano Shrine. In his vision, he was told that all the Shinto Deities are just the radiance of Amida Buddha's compassion. Therefore, devotion to Amida Buddha and chanting the name of Amida Buddha was the deepest aspect of Shinto, according to his tradition. All other Shinto rites were, in essence, skillful displays of the nembutsu. Kakuban and Shinran, two major figures of Pure Land Buddhism, would develop ideas similar to this around the same time period. Kakuban and Shinran would go on to form an Esoteric Pure Land tradition which also synthesized Shinto as a magical display of the esoteric nature of the nembutsu. But, I digress.

After having this vision, Genji Yorimitsu taught this Hijutsu to his retainers and they, through a series of events, found the cannibal thieves. Posing as Yamabushi who had broken their vows, they entered into the hideout. While inside, the group poisoned the cannibal leaders, then commenced a full on assault, killing all but a few of the cannibals. They then rescued the surviving girls and took record of the name of those who they had found dead, partially eaten, or had learned about from the surviving girls. The group then guided the women back to Kyoto, reuniting the survivors with their families and presenting the Imperial Court with the names of the deceased. The operation was considered a success and Genji Yorimitsu and his retainers were well rewarded.

Thus, according to the oral tradition, this was the first time that the Hachiman Daibosatsu tradition of Hijutsu/Ninjutsu was used. This tradition, allegedly, serves as the foundation for the shinobi-no-jutsu later found in the House of Nojiri.

Again, I must stress to the reader that this origin story is oral tradition and I have no documentation to prove that it connects back to the 990s, or even the 1300s. As such, take it with caution. We see that many shinobi traditions, in the Edo period, seem to be picking various historical and mythological events and inserting a ninjutsu origin into those stories. This origin story may very well be just that-- a creation at a later date.

However, I have presented it to provide it due to the symbolism it contains and the messages it presents.

CHAPTER 2

Preliminary Details

The Origin of Fukushima Ryu

Simply put, the origin of Fukushima Ryu Ninjutsu is the House of Nojiri, which can also be identified as the House of Kumazawa. On a day somewhere between 1600 and 1610, Nojiri Narimasa sat down and wrote the Fukushima Ryu Shinobi no Maki. However, the Fukushima Ryu came into existence prior to the manual being written. The general understanding is that the system was formed when the House of Fukushima was awarded the Hiroshima area as reward for their role at the Battle of Sekigahara. There is also some logic to suggest that the system existed prior to this movement of the House of Fukushima to Hiroshima. Theories aside, we know that Nojiri Narimasa wrote the manual in the Hiroshima area sometime between 1600 and 1610, with the estimate hovering around 1602. The actual starting date of the system, and the year the manual was written, is now seemingly lost to history. Even my own family does not know the actual start or pen dates. However, tradition suggests the system's start date cannot have been before 1595. Based on the context and material within the manual, it seems logical and rational to assume that the system was based on material stemming from Kusunoki Ryu and Go-Nancho (Southern Court) loyalists, and that the system was not formally codified into Fukushima Ryu until the turn of the century (between 1595-1610). Tradition holds that the manual was penned in Hiroshima, and thus, the start date for the manual must be after 1600.

In summary, the family tradition and historical evidence supports the theory that techniques from the Southern Court loyalists were reorganized into Fukushima Ryu by Nojiri Narimasa sometime between 1595 and 1602 and the manual was written around 1602.

Inko Ryu

We also know that a system of ninjutsu, named "Inko Ryu" shares much of the same magic with Fukushima Ryu. This relationship is established by a pair of documents written in 1774. One is an Inko Ryu manual and the other is a third Fukushima Ryu manual. The two documents are, essentially, copies of each other, just with different names. However, in terms of historical timeline, the Fukushima Ryu Shinobi-no-maki dates from in-between 1595-1610, making it ~165 years older than these two documents. As such, Fukushima Ryu is, as per the historical timeline, older and thus predates Inko Ryu.

In a previous work, I had said that the House of Fujii established Inko Ryu. However, upon further investigation into Inko Ryu, it has become clear that the House of Fujii's ninjutsu's name maybe lost to history. All of the historical evidence compels one to conclude that Inko Ryu was created in the late 1600s, perhaps early 1700s. While there are some ninjutsu historians that claim an earlier date, there exists no evidence that I have seen to compel me to assume a date earlier than the 1600s. As such, it is the stance of the author that Fukushima Ryu predates Inko Ryu and that Inko Ryu was formed at a later date. It is even plausible that Inko Ryu was formed by an offshoot of Fukushima Ryu students.

Serving as Chief Retainers

The leader of the House of Fukushima was Fukushima Daiyu Masanori, a samurai from the Owari area who many historians believe to be a cousin to Toyotomi Hideyoshi. Fukushima Masanori and Toyotomi were both born and raised in the Nagoya area. This is the same area the House of Nojiri lived and operated in while in service to Oda Nobunaga. In the early 1500s, the Nojiri were based out of the Iimori area of Kawachi Province and the Hibitsu area of Owari (modern day Nagoya). However, by the late 1500s, Oda Nobunaga was dead and the Nojiri were no longer in Kawachi, only the Hibitsu area of Owari. At this time, the Nojiri were serving the House of Toyotomi. It was at this time, as is understood, that the Nojiri came to serve the House of Fukushima.

For a keen understanding of the series of events taking place in the late 1500s, in regard to the House of Nojiri, it is critical to remember that the House of Nojiri was also the House of Kumazawa. Oda Nobunaga had allowed the Southern Court loyalists and the authentic Emperor to reside, without any interference, in a town called Sebe (modern day Ichinomiya, Aichi Prefecture). This town is located just slightly north of the Hibitsu area of Owari. This is a key piece of information, because it shows that Oda Nobunaga had some kind of respect for the Southern Court Loyalists, as he did not demand anything from them, nor did he interfere with their activities. In fact, the original seat of Oda's power, Kiyosu, rests in-between Hibitsu and Sebe. While Oda did not interfere, he most likely kept a keen eye on the Southern Court activities.

However, with mounting political and economic pressures, the Southern Court Emperor and the princes were forced to eventually enter into service of feudal lords. The House of Kumazawa/Nojiri made careful plans to place their members into a careful web of influential lords. For the most part, the House of Nojiri/Kumazawa focused the majority of their efforts into Oda Nobunaga. The service was initially spread out among direct service to Oda Nobunaga and service to two of Oda's main generals, Sakuma and Shibata. When the House of Sakuma was disgraced, that line of influence spread to Oda Nobukatsu.

[Hereafter, whenever "House of Nojiri" is mentioned, the reader is to understand that "House of Nojiri" means the Nojiri and Kumazawa. In historical records, this group is identified as both the House of Nojiri and/or the House of Kumazawa. Either way implies both the Nojiri and Kumazawa families.]

When Oda Nobunaga died, the safety of Sebe began to dissolve and the House of Nojiri had to rely on their service to other feudal lords to maintain a level of income and resources. The House of Nojiri had been situated in the House of Shibata, House of Nakagawa, House of Oda Nobukatsu, and the House of Toyotomi. However, the Battle of Shizugatake, being a political nightmare, threw much of this into disarray. The House of Shibata fell and the Nojiri serving the House of Nakagawa died. After this battle, there was a significant amount of shifting and powerful struggles over the next few years. In the end, the House of Nojiri consolidated the majority of its efforts behind the House of Toyotomi, which led to service in the House of Fukushima. The service which brought the Nojiri to the House of Fukushima came through, primarily, the Kumazawa line.

An important historical note needs to be made here. The Kumazawa imperial princes had been protected by the Nojiri line for years. This extended even into marriage and adoptions. Some of the Nojiri line were actually born from the Kumazawa line and adopted into the Nojiri line. These marriages and adoptions are what made the House of Nojiri and House of Kumazawa a single unit. For example, Nojiri Shoken Muneyasu was born from the Kumazawa line and adopted by the Nojiri line. During this time, Nojiri Muneyasu controlled the Kawachi operations and Nojiri Yoshikage controlled the Owari operations. However, by the 1570s, both lines merged and focused their power in Owari. This unified effort was controlled by men such as Nojiri Shigemasa. By the 1590s, the House of Nojiri began to serve House of Fukushima.

Kumazawa Morihisa was a close retainer to Fukushima Masanori. In fact, Kumazawa Morihisa maintained service with Fukushima Masanori until Masanori's death. Due to this close retainer relationship, Fukushima Masanori decided to entrust the espionage of the House of Fukushima, and all applicable retainers, to the teachings and techniques of the House of Nojiri. Nojiri Narimasa was selected to organize and lead this system during its infancy. Sometime after, Narimasa wrote the Fukushima Ryu Shinobi no Maki.

Fukushima Ryu is not Iga Ryu

It is both over simplified and inaccurate to say that Fukushima Ryu is rooted in Iga ryu, as many researchers and historians have done. While many of Fukushima Ryu's teachings appeared to be rooted in the Iga traditions, such an assumption is looking at history from the wrong direction. As explained previously, the material is more likely to have come from Kusunoki Ryu and other related Go-Nancho (Southern Court) systems. While it is true that the Iga region received a good amount of Kusunoki Ryu, much of this material was uncredited by war manual writers of the early 1600s. Many authors erroneously viewed the material as originating in Iga, when it really originated in Kusunoki Ryu (or other Go-Nancho systems).

Since the House of Nojiri has a rich history in the Osaka and Nara areas, had interaction with Kusunoki Ryu figures, and is part of the Go-Nancho, it would further seem logical that the material is sourced from a Go-Nancho origin, not an Iga origin.

Why, then, do some historians claim the system is Iga Ryu?

Those historians lack an understanding of the history.

The Murakami family was the last family within the main line of the tradition. This main line was kept alive by the House of Fukushima after the Nojiri had ceased service. That is, the Murakami family, serving the House of Fukushima in the Nagano area, formally presided over the "official" transmission of the system. It is possible that they, in the 1800s, may have identified it as Iga Ryu. However, beyond being pure speculation, there are three key problems with this possible claim:

1.) History shows us that the material is most likely sourced from Go-Nancho origins.
2.) The annotations to the manual, written in 1797, show a handful of errors. While the annotations were not written by the Murakami themselves, the errors in the manual evidence a degeneration of the material. This means that any claim to Iga Ryu, in the late 1700s, could be equally erroneous.
3.) It became popular for shinobi traditions to trace their origins back to Iga or Koka during the Edo period. Traditions that had no claim to such origins were simply given those origins in order to sound important. This led to the erroneous idea that all shinobi traditions came from Iga or Koka, which is simply not true. Unfortunately, many present day historians, for various reasons, continue to push this erroneous idea.

The Nojiri, presently, do not identify the system as Iga Ryu. My branch of the family clearly operates off the idea that the system was descended from the Southern Court Loyalists and their tactics. I, the author, also consider the system to be a descendant branch of Kusunoki Ryu (see the Kusunoki Ryu Addendum).

Furthermore, there are no historical documents (pre-Meiji) that I am aware of which connect Fukushima Ryu to Iga Ryu. It seems the connectionis purely a modern day mistake.

The Magic

The magic in the system is rooted heavily magic from Ise and western Owari. Specifically, the magic coming from the Ise Shrine

(Shinto), Shingon inspired material, Taoism and material from the esoteric Pureland tradition. The traces of Shingon stem from the Kusunoki Ryu influence and from the Shingon temples around Kawachi. There is additional commentary, concerning the magic, in the Conclusion of this book.

Fukushima Shinobi-no-Maki

The Fukushima Shinobi no Maki is a teaching spread over five scrolls. The first four scrolls are a seemingly random collection of magical techniques, weaponry, and tools. The fifth volume contains a short but profound closing statement from Nojiri Narimasa. The five volumes, in all reality, contain very little information in terms of actual written material. The manual serves as a catalogue of a collection of specific tools, magic, and basic principles. To be more accurate, we should say that the manual is not meant to be an instructional guide, but rather, and reminder (a memory aide) of specifically selected items.

Even if the reader doesn't believe my words, they need merely to read the manual (or translation at least) themselves. Upon reading the manual, it is painfully obvious that much of the teaching has been left out of the scrolls.

The Fukushima Ryu Shinobi no Maki's Annotations were written by Terasawa Sensei in 1797 (almost 200 years later). **Being ~190 years the junior, the Annotations do contain verifiable errors in some places.**

The annotations state that the items in the manual were specifically recorded by Nojiri Narimasa due to directives given by Fukushima Masanori. Whether this is true or not is impossible to tell, but it may explain why some techniques were catalogued and other techniques were not. I am of the belief that the material is a set of memory aides of specifically selected items. As the final scrolls suggest, there is an entire body of knowledge, technique, and training not included in the scrolls.

Thus, it seems the Fukushima Ryu Shinobi no Maki is a collection of the more magical and tool-related aspects of the system, allegedly selected by Fukushima Masanori himself, to appear in a short memory aide.

The language of the final scroll suggests that the five scrolls would be given to the student once they achieved a level of competency. As it seems, the student would be trained to be a ninshi and then be given the document once they achieved a high enough status in the training. The document would serve more of a ceremonial function than an actual instructional function. This is a rational assumption, as many of manuals from the time period served the dual function of memory aid and proof of study (graduation document).

Author's Interruption

Now, as the author, I must ask the reader to take a moment and read the following section.

According to Nojiri tradition: The teachings which were specifically left out of the manual were the teachings related to the "covert diplomacy" aspect of shinobi-no-jutsu. We know, from the Southern Court material, and specific branches of Kusunoki Ryu, that there existed extensive teachings related to the "covert diplomacy" arts.

These were often referred by such names as Haka-no-Mono ("Conspirator"), Mistudan ("Covert Conversations") and Kyodan (loosely translated as 'Feasting on Gossip" or 'Speech Eater'). We know that the *Bansenshukai* records Oda Nobunaga calling his shinobi "Kyodan", which evidences that Oda Nobunaga may have had many Southern Court Loyalists and/or Kusunoki Ryu trained shinobi in his service. Considering the amount of confirmed Southern Court Loyalists and Kusunoki Ryu trained retainers Oda Nobunaga had in his services, this assumption seems to be a sound one. Considering that it is historically verified that Oda Nobunaga had men such s Kusunoki Masatora, Nojiri Hanbei, Nojiri Muneyasu, Kumazawa Morihisa, etc. in his service (either directly or serving a chief retainer), it would almost seem irrational to assume he did not utilize their clandestine skills.

Interestingly enough, we do see some possible overlap with Iga material at this point. This overlap, however, does not entail origin or transmission. Some Iga mono studied Kusunoki Ryu as well.

We know the Kusunoki main line and a branch of the Hattori served Oda Nobunaga. The Kusunoki family of Kawachi were connected, by marriages, to the Hattori of the Iga area. These marriages may be the source of transmission of many Kusunoki and Southern Court clandestine arts appearing in Iga material. *The Iga Scroll of Yorihide*, inherited by Chikamatsu Shigenori in the 1700s, contains some of this information. The final chapters of the *Shinobi Hiden* also seem to discuss some of this material. The *Bansenshukai*, originally a work predominately of Iga origin (but heavily dispersed through Koka Ryu systems), contains a considerable amount of the "covert diplomacy" teachings. In fact, the Bansenshukai seems to reference Kusunoki Ryu material more than any other system. One could almost argue that the *Bansenshukai* is really Kusunoki Ryu in disguise!

I would advise the reader to consult the *Bansenshukai* for more of the actual shinobi-no-mono skills which are not addressed within the Fukushima Ryu Shinobi-no-Maki.

All of this said, the Fukushima Ryu Shinobi no Maki contains very little information by itself. It does, however, serve as an excellent guidebook. As you can see from this book you are reading, there is an immense amount of commentary and explanation for this small and seemingly simply collection of scrolls.

The final scroll contains a short passage heavily infused with multiple layers of meaning. The final scroll, which I choose to translate into English as "*Scroll of Refining the Intention*" serves as the short and esoteric teaching of all the material previously left out. That is, the final scroll contains the essence of the "covert diplomacy" teachings in a short and simple presentation. The meaning is not spelled out in any kind of detail. Most if the meaning is simply hidden within the inferences made by Nojiri Narimasa.

Furthermore, the final scroll of the manual serves as the foundational view and heart teaching of the entire system. Whenever any public commentary is given on the Fukushima Ryu Shinobi no Maki, it really should start with the final scroll. It sets the entire view and tone for the entire system. I was torn, when writing this book, on whether or not to put the scroll first or last. I have kept it last to maintain the format of the original root text.

Since the majority of the material was selected by, according to oral tradition, Fukushima Masanori, we see that the final scroll is Nojiri Narimasa's words of caution. Since the manual was a collection of magic and tools, we get the impression that the final scroll is Nojiri's words of caution to anyone reading the manual. That is, Nojiri intends for the reader to clearly understand that this scroll is only showcasing magic and specialized tools. The actual art of espionage and the proper mind training is not contained in the manual. As such, Nojiri gives this brief teaching to warn and guide any readers towards the actual heart of the material.

In the final teaching of the manual, Nojiri Narimasa saves the heart essence of the entire manual for the last lines of teaching. The heart of the entire system, and as Nojiri Narimasa says, the heart of all victories, is simply:

"The key Principle is Shunyata."

Thus, with this in mind, let us begin the commentary on the Fukushima Ryu Shinobi no Maki.

CHAPTER 3

The Fukushima Ryu Shinobi-no-Maki

Commentary by Steven Nojiri

The Combined Collection
(Fukushima Ryu Ninjutsu no Sho)

When you combine the original manual with the Annotations, the collection is referred as the "Fukushima Ryu Ninjutsu no Sho". We will begin with the actual Shinobi no Maki, written by Nojiri Narimasa. When finished with this, we will move to the Annotations written by Terasawa Sensei.

"Fukushima Ryu Shinobi no Maki"

Scroll 1

The root text does not have any introduction. However, the Annotations do have a segment. That segment states:

"This document is a collection of techniques chosen by Lord Fukushima. Shinobi is a type of spy and spies are employed in order

*to obtain information about the enemy. This is so that you can
determine which of the enemy's plans are real and which are false.*

*This will allow you to gain victory in any conflict. Espionage is a
critical matter*

*Sun Tzu's Tactics say:
'Without subtle ingenuity of mind, one cannot make certain of the
truth of the spy's reports. It is subtle! Subtle! Usage of spies extends
to every kind of activity.' "*

While the main text has no opening, this opening of the Annotations
is important because it establishes four important points.

1.) That Fukushima Masanori chose the material to be included in
the root text. This line supports the oral tradition that Nojiri
Narimasa went over the system with Fukushima Masanori and that
Masanori selected the techniques to place in the document. As such,
this further supports the idea that the manual is a type of "graduation
document", viewable to those who have studied and mastered the
material to the point of learning the items contained within the
document.

2.) The line "Shinobi is a type of spy" needs to be explained. The
wording of the original Japanese implies that the shinobi and the
other spies are of one group, yet it clearly demarcates the shinobi
from the other spies. In fact, the kanji used (義) is a very interesting
choice of wording. Normally, it would mean "morality or virtue".
However, within grammatical context, it means *"something
equivalent, but not exactly the same"*. While the shinobi is a spy,
there is something distinct which makes the shinobi not exactly
equivalent to a spy. The reason for this is that shinobi, while being a
type of spy, is associated with the "Living Spy". That is, the shinobi
is sent by their lord to go into enemy territory and recruit local
commoners and local retainers to serve as spies. The entire group
becomes one network of spies. However, the shinobi is distinctly
different because he is loyal and serving his master, while the other
spies are actually disloyal and have betrayed their lord. This
ideology is rooted in Kusunoki Ryu (See the Kusunoki Ryu
Addendum for an explanation of these two types of spies), and

further back, is rooted in text such as the *Six Secret Teachings* and the *Sun Tzu Tactics*.

3.) The shinobi are used to determine which of the enemy's plans are real or fake. This can also mean a determination of which plans are viable and which plans are just ideas. As you will see in the final scroll of the root text, Nojiri Narimasa references the third chapter of the *Sun Tzu Tactics* which states that the highest form of warfare is to severe the enemy's plans, that is, to attack and dismantle their plans (伐謀).

4.) The quote from the *Sun Tzu Tactics* is classic and reminds us all that the use of espionage is a subtle matter that extends to all things.

夢相通
Interlocking Dreams

The first scroll opens with a spell for influencing dreams. The name of this spell, 夢相通, roughly translates to "Interlocking with Dreams". This is an old paper spell with roots in the Ise region, specifically, the Grand Ise Shrine. A variation of this spell also exists in Inko Ryu Ninjutsu. As a variation, of course, the Inko Ryu version has slightly different instructions.

The use of paper spells is very common in Nojiri methods. To this day, we have several paper spells within our family traditions. We also have many paper spell alternatives to some of the more brutal spells found in some of the shinobi traditions.

For example, the method of starving and murdering a dog in order to create a dog spirit servant (Inu-Kami "dog deity") is replaced in the Nojiri methodology by the use of origami-like paper dogs (Inu-Gami "Dog-Paper") used to channel already deceased dog-spirits. Also, as you will see later, there is a spell involving the eyes of a dog contained in a crimson cloth bag. A variation of this spell exists in other systems. In those systems, you must rip the eyes from a living dog. However, in the Fukushima Ryu, there is some variation. In Fukushima Ryu, one can take the eyes from a dead dog as well.

Dog magic is complicated and very powerful. It actually holds a special place in many cultures around the world, not just Japanese magic. It is advised that only well trained and seasoned infiltrators attempt any such magic.

This "Interlocking Dream" spell is also "Cemetery Magic", meaning that it is relies upon ghosts. Therefore, it is not something to be taken lightly.

In fact, I flat out advise that the reader do not attempt any of the spells (or poisons, as seen later) that appear in this manual.

The root text says:

"Interlocking Dreams
- *On the 14ᵗʰ and/or the 15th fifteenth day of the seventh month, collect 2 momme of pine wood charcoal which has been burnt around a grave*
- *Take 5 bu of moss from a grave*
- *Gather dew that from the leaves of a Taro plant which is growing to the east of your own house*
- *Charred Newt. Male or Female. Kuden.*
- *Your own earwax. Mix the ingredients into an ink. Kuden"*

The 14ᵗʰ and 15ᵗʰ day of the Seventh (Lunar) Month is the Hungry Ghost Festival. This is critical because this dream spell, as stated earlier, is related to ghosts. The entire seventh lunar month is considered a month for spirits and ghosts. In fact, a spell that will come later in the text also requires ingredients gathered during "ghost month". It should also be noted that the 14/15ᵗʰ is the Full Moon. The pine charcoal is related to the various offerings which take place during this time period.

The taro plant is also known as "elephant ears". The leaves are very large and a considerable amount of dew is collected from the leaves.

Below are the diagrams from the manual, showing the finalized spell.

This diagram is of the paper spell prepare and folded.
The Seimei and Doman seals are marked on the diagram.
The item below the spell is the Willow Brush

Now, this is all that is revealed out in the manual. As the manual itself is simply meant to serve as a catalog and memory aid. For more information, we turn to the Annotations.

The Annotation say:

"   *Interlocking dreams is a document that causes your enemy's dreams to be disrupted. Gather used charcoal of pine wood that has been used at a grave. Any grave will do. The grave moss can also be from any grave. When gathering dew from taro leaves, write 伊 on the leaves and then collect the dew. The next ingredient is newt and the oral tradition for this explains that, if the intended target of the spell is male, then use a female newt. When distinguishing if a newt is male or female, know that male newts have a blue belly. Female newts have a red belly. Concerning this tradition of the newt: Capture male and female newts when they are mating and separate them. Next, put these newts into a bamboo tube, but put them in separate internodes, with a node keeping them apart. Close the openings and leave them for three days. After three days, you will find that the newts have chewed through the node, making a hole in the node. Take the newts out. They will be joined in copulation. Separate the newts again. Char them separately. The target's sex will determine which newt you need to use.*

To make the ink: Powder four of the ingredients. Then, finalize the mixture by adding the dew you collected from the Taro leaves. When rubbing the ink stick (to make ink), any pottery will work. However, you must use pure water.

The brush should be made from the Weeping Willow. Write down the specifics (regarding your target). Before you use the brush, write 伊 on the brush. The way to finalize the letter is the same way of making "tied letters". Draw the Seal of Seimei on the knot. Then, place the Seal of Doman on the bottom. Write the target's name on the top and then put your name below it. If there is a sea or a river around the gates, write 舟 ("ship") on the underside of the spell. This letter should then be placed in any graveyard."

Terasawa Sensei is correct, but this needs some refinement. It is not that male newts are always blue bellied. The male newt becomes blue bellied during the mating season and when they are sexually charged. The fact that you need to have the newts when they are in their mating season is a key factor in the spell. What is not said in the manual or the annotations is that part of the magic of the spell relies on the sexual energy of the two newts prior to be killed. There is meaning within the (cruel) manipulation of the newts during their breeding period. In so many ways, the sexual energy is residual in their charred remains. Due to the nature of this ingredient, it can be exchanged for a less cruel ingredient for those interested in an alternative ingredient.

Also, while your own earwax may seem an odd ingredient, it is similar to adding your own spit. Believe it or not, human spit can often time be food to ghosts and beings in lower realms. If you don't believe this, watch as even dogs sometimes go to eat your spit. Even a dog that is well nourished will often try to eat the spit of particular people. This effect is multiplied even further by ghosts. Spit, snot, ear wax, etc. As odd as it sounds, the addition of your earwax is a form of food offering.

The items taken from the cemetery have their own magical properties, and as the manual says, this should all be mixed to create an ink.

For the willow brush, you must make it a double ended brush. One end is a point with a hollow section, like any classical ink pen. The other end is a brush made from the fibers of the willow. You do not add anything further to achieve this brush, simply cut the end numerous times until it produces a brush like effect.

You have to write the kanji 伊 onto the brush. The reason for this is directly tied to the belief that the Ise (伊勢)Shrine is sacred and that you want to connect the sacred power of the Ise Shrine to your brush. Furthermore, the kanji itself is composed of the meaning of "people" and "to direct/order". When joined together, in the old days, it meant a symbol uniting the Gods and the People in directed and ordered harmony. Specifically, it was meant to be a stamp/seal of approval of the Sun Deity Amaterasu. Thus, with this context, one can understand the shrine of Ise to mean "Shrine of Amaterasu's Energy and Strength". In fact, even the famous region of Iga's name is involved in this meaning. "Iga" means "Amaterasu's Joy", within this context. Therefore, you write the kanji 伊 on the brush to connect it to this source of power.

Furthermore, you write the Seal of Seimei (Five Point Star) and the Seal of Doman (Nine Slash Grid) on the paper spell. This also is Ise magic. The Seal of Seimei is not a mysterious or shrouded in mystery symbol. It traces directly back to a man named Abe no Seimei, a sorcerer from early Japanese history who resided in the Ise area. In fact, his essence is said to be retained in the Ise Shrine as well. He used the five point star to increase the power of his spells and to increase the power of his verbal curses and prayers. From that point on, practitioners of Ise region magic have used the Five Point Star to increase the power of a spell.

The Seal of Doman (the nine slash grid) is commonly understood by people to simply point to Kuji Kiri magic. While Kuji Kiri magic is absolutely part of the Seal of Doman, it too has a specific origin. It traces back to Abe no Seimei's chief rival, Ashiya Doman. This sorcerer used the Nine Slash grid to expel and exorcise demons and dangerous ghost. Even though, historically, Abe no Seimei ultimately proved himself to be stronger than Ashiya Doman, the two's legacies became intertwined in the Ise region and the combination of the Seal of Seimei and the Seal of Doman became a standard magical practice. When the two seals are combined, it is believed that it empowers the spell and protects it from being influenced or effected by evil spirits and vengeful ghost.

It should also be mentioned that Abe no Seimei is, in legend, half spirit himself and that his methods were considered ultimately stronger because of this. Legends also mention that he could control weak spirits without any magic, just by his commands. Both Abe no Seimei and Ashiya Doman were Onmyodo adepts.

As such, this paper spell is, essentially, an Onmyodo spell.

To finalize the spell, the letter is placed back in the graveyard. If there are rivers, lakes, or any major body of water nearby (between the graveyard and your target), you need to write the kanji for boat on the back of the spell. This provides the ability for the spell to be taken out past the water, as many spirits cannot pass openly on the open water. By applying the command 'boat' to the spell, you provide the ghost the permission and ability to cross over water.

Remember, paper spells are like an order ticket which you present to the spirit world. You write your request (sometime in code, sometime plainly) and then you seal and bind the spell, properly. When done correctly, particular spirits will receive the orders and carry them out. This is why it is important to put the Seal of Seimei and the Seal of Doman on the spells, as you do not want any vengeful ghost getting involved. Once the spirit has the order, the spell provides them with directives and also provides them with permissions (such as 'boat') to carry out the task. In exchange, they must have access to something they want. In this case, the ghosts get to consume the essence of the materials in the ink. As many ghosts are essence and smell eaters, the materials are very worthwhile for them.

Of course, a more full and complete explanation of this spell is more complicated than I have explained in this commentary. However, the above explanation is a decent beginning.

下馬落
Knocking Horses Down

This spell is meant to cause discord between the horse and the rider. In particular, it is meant to cause the horse to buck the rider off continuously.

Although the purpose of the spell is to knock a rider off of the horse, the spell actually attacks the horse.

The spell, when prepared, looks like this:

The prepared spell
Take note of the Seal of Seimei and Seal of Doman.
A special brush is used for this spell as well.

The main text shows the picture and says:

"

逢坂ヤ八坂サカ中鯖一サシ行基ニクレテ駒ヤハラヤム

There is a considerable amount of kuden regarding this spell."

Furthermore, the Annotations say:

"The spell is to cause problems with the enemy's horse.
Pull a piece of wood from a torii's horizontal beam and form a
toothpick from this wood. Then, write 伊 for Ise (伊勢) three times on
toothpick.

Create a paper envelope, similar to medicine packages. Write the enemy's name on the front of the envelope with the Seal of Doman, the Seal of Seimei, and write your own name. Dig a hole next to the hoof print of the enemy's horse and bury the package. Also, remember to bury the toothpick with the spell. When this is done, the horse will fall over and undergo hardships.

To end this trouble, chant this poem. Then, dig up and retrieve the buried items: 逢坂ヤ八坂坂中鯖一差行基ニクレテ駒ハイサナン

At this the horse will immediately recover."

One key detail is to remember that you do not dig up the horse's track itself. Rather, you dig to the side of the track and then dig underneath the track. The spell is then placed underneath the track, and the track stays intact

The Nojiri also have to more spells related to this spell. One is a mixture of special plants mixed with spit and placed into the track of the horse. This spell affects the horse's speed. The other spell is a paper spell that is violently popped open, at the right time, to influence the rider to fall from the horse. Neither of these two versions appears in this scroll, however.

Furthermore, it is important to write 伊 on the piece of wood that you have taken form the torii. This is for the same reason as in the Interlocking Dream spell. This helps to channel the power of the Ise Shrine into the writing implement.

For those who are unfamiliar with torii, you should know that torii is an aspect of Shinto. The torii gates mark any place where kami reside. Therefore, the wood of the torii gate will be magically potent because the torii is the gateway between the mundane territory and the abode of a kami.

It is important to know that sacred things are actually sacred. In these modern times, too many people dismiss sacred objects or sacred space and the world is worse off for this type of view. There are many objects which have magical properties. Many potent spells exist which are the combination of ingredients which people mistakenly believe have no magical powers. One example is a spell where you take ashes of a priest who performed fire offerings (that is, a priest who was specialized in fire offerings) and you make a small bag to hold his ashes. This bag, when worn on your body, will help to make you invisible to enemies. Furthermore, one can wear various things in their hair or on their head to make them invisible, such as amulets and even viper fangs.

The reason this works is because of "Interdependent Origination"— that is, all things arise from causes and all things serve as causes. Everything is related. Within this web of relationships, some things are potent and "magical". When things are very potent in this way, we say that those things are sacred. When we reject the idea of sacredness or magic, we are rejecting the idea of interdependence and we rob ourselves of the rich experience of interacting with the sacred. The torii represents this boundary between mundane and magical. So, Nojiri Narimasa is saying to believe in the sacred and take a piece of the torii to write the spell.

It is also important to understand that the chant to break this spell relies on the power of Gyoki, a very important Buddhist monk during the 700s. He is also known as Gyoki Bosatsu. Gyoki spent much of his life wandering Japan and establishing Dharma centers for the lay practitioners to gather and practice. This was unusual at the time because most monks were only establishing official temples. Gyoki was establishing local centers, not temples. This activity made him unpopular with the government for a period of time, as all of his work was unofficial and unsanctioned. Eventually though, Gyoki donated a large portion of his time to civil engineering projects for the Imperial Palace, drawing up some of the first maps of Japan. It should be noted that Gyoki envisioned Japan as a single pointed vajra. Gyoki passed away in the late 700s. While his official resting site is in Nara Prefecture, his presence is heavily felt in the Kyoto area.

The Yasaka Hill, mentioned in the chant, is in the Kyoto area. Thus, to break this curse, one simply visualizes and verbalizes that they are making a food offering to Gyoki Bosatsu and the curse is lifted.

村雨明松
The "Murasame" Torch

This main text says:
"

- 'Flower' – 10 momme
- Camphor – 7 momme
- Pine – 10 momme 5 bu"

The Annotations say:

"This is torch is resistant to the rain. "Flower" means the Anise tree. Soak this wood in water for 100 days before you powder it. "Pine" means resin saturated pine wood. The second ingredient is camphor. The three ingredients should be turned into fine powder. This mixture should be put into a paper bag and then wrapped in 6 or 7 layers of paper. This is done to prevent the fire from extinguished."

There is not a lot to say beyond what has been written. The torch, being made from various pine pieces, with some camphor, burns well. The value of torches is very vague in the mind of modern day people, due to our abundance of electric lights and lighters. Fire and illumination are taken for granted, and the value of various torches is not perceived.

In these modern times, it may seem that such a torch is mostly just a reminder of the cultural legacy. However, it is possible that in various woodland scenarios you may have the opportunity to build and use a torch such as this, so it is a good idea to learn the basics. I would suggest using a torch such as this rather than relying on just your lighter or flashlight. The lesson here is "resource management". Don't use all fuel in your lighter or all the batteries in your flashlight. Make a torch to conserve resources.

Use a lighter to ignite the torch, but then save the fuel and flint and allow the natural process of the flame to provide you with the needed heat and illumination. So, if you have a flashlight, then that is good. However, you want to conserve it for times when a torch is not available. If you only have a lighter, you can produce a simple torch (such as this) and get a lot of return for very little investment.

The image of the torch as provided in the main text.

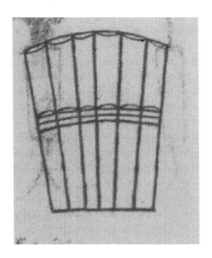

打明松
The Strike Torch

The strike torch is the same essential idea as the previous torch, but it is intended to be deployed as opposed to being carried. As the text says, if you add the spikes, the torch can be planted without much effort.

The main text says:
"

-   *Camphor – 10 momme*
-   *Saltpetre – 9 momme*
-   *Sulphur – 3 momme*
-   *'Flower' – 10 momme*

More details in the oral tradition"

The Annotations say:

"

- *Camphor -10 momme*
- *Saltpetre -9 momme*
- *Sulphur -3 momme*
- *Anise wood soaked in water for 100 days – 10 momme*
- *Pine Wood soaked in resin - 9 momme and 1 bu"*

Prepare this in the same manner as the above "Murasame" torch. If you situate spikes in a criss-cross form and throw it, it will land correctly and burn well."

Again, this balance between cultural heritage and modern day application is a balancing act. However, as it is not useless to know many various techniques, you should learn and consider this technique. A day may come where it will be needed.

Image of the Strike-Torch:

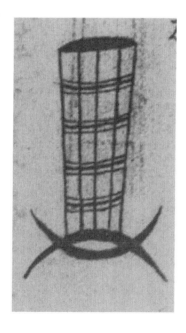

Furthermore, even if one never needs to use such a torch in a real life-and-death situation, it is good to learn for the historical and cultural value. This is especially important for anyone who studies the shinobi path as a form of maintaining traditions of the past (out of curiousity or obligation).

The famous ninja manual, *Shoninki*, mentions that shinobi will recognize each other by the torches they use. In this way, if you learn how to properly make and use the torches mentioned in this manual, then others can recognize that you have been exposed to Fukushima Ryu.

タ〃ミ橋
Folding Bridge/Ladder

The main text simply provides this picture:

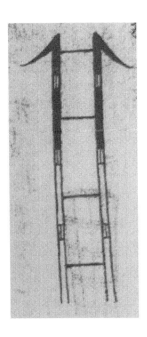

Beyond that, the Annotations say:

"This ladder is used when crossing over moats and similar situations. This ladder is constructed so that it can be folded, making it less difficult to use. It has hinges so that it can be extended. It has hinges and metal latches to lock it in place. Furthermore, you can attach a thin rope to the end of the ladder, which has a three pronged grapple on the end, and use it to climb up."

Even though this topic is breezed over in the manual, there is quite a lot of material contained in the unspoken/unwritten portion of the teaching. Ladders and bridges are a major portion of the shinobi methodology. Shinobi no mono relied on various types of ladders and bridges to scale not only over walls, but across gaps (such as one roof to the next roof).

Many other shinobi manuals, such as the *Bansenshukai* and the *Shinobi Hiden* have more extensive written records of the ladders and bridges. The reader of the main text is not meant to see a single ladder and assume that is the only ladder. The mention of the ladder is a memory aid to remind the student of ALL the ladders/bridges and their functions. Nojiri Narimasa used many memory aids throughout the main text.

In particular, it is important to understand that, in this system, ladders are deployed horizontally just as much, if not more, than vertically. One need only look at modern day firefighting to see this horizontal usage of ladders. Modern day firefighting uses this exact ladder in the picture, even calling it a "hooked ladder". The hooks are not meant to grab onto the edge of a wall or ledge, but rather, they are meant to hook onto the backside of architecture while the ladder is used as a bridge. This ladder is also hooked to the apex of a roof and the ladder becomes an aid for walking up the roof line. This ladder is also hooked and lodged into position to serve as a platform so that shinobi can do work while suspended high above the world below.

Also, as the commentary mentions, this ladder can also be deployed to cross over creeks and streams. Beyond this, one can deploy a grappling hook and then connect the ladder to the rope, thus creating vertical movement.

鋸
Saws

Another such memory aid is the simple mention of a saw. The main text shows only the following picture:

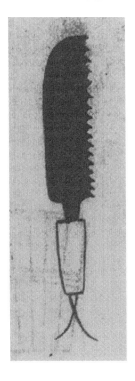

The Annotations simply say:

"Saws have many purposes and this tradition has many oral traditions."

Again, this does not mean that the above saw is the only saw. It means that the above saw is the primary saw. The 'dove tail pull saw' pattern is the main pattern for the Fukushima Ryu. However, it is not the only saw available to Fukushima Ryu practitioners.

As is the standard purpose of saws in ninjutsu, this saw is used to break into a location. Many of the doors/windows of old Japan were locked with wooden bolts. If the shinobi was not in a situation where he needed to avoid signs of forced entry, he could simply use a small pry-bar to expose access to the bolt and then use this thin pull saw to cut the bolt. Once the bolt is cut, the door/window will open.

The saw would also be used to cut lattice work away from access points and even, in some instances, be used to cut portions of fencing off. Cutting away small portions of window bars, lattice work, or even minor pieces of architecture would provide the shinobi with a gap to insert lock picking/by-passing tools. These small bits of removed architecture may even possibly go unnoticed until days later. If no one ever specifically comes looking (investigating the break-in), the removed parts may go undetected indefinitely.

As the Annotations say, saws have many purposes and there is a considerable amount of tradition regarding saws. One other such usage would be using a saw to dismantle barriers that have been put up, or vice-versa, used to cut architecture away for usage in building barriers.

錐
Drill

The main text only shows the following picture:

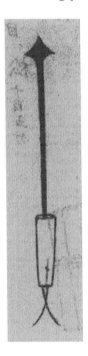

The Annotations are silent on this matter.

Again, this image serves as a memory aid. Various types of picks and drills are used in Fukushima Ryu. This image is only the basic design. Drills and picks have many uses, all of them related to breaking-and-entering. In old Japan, the shinobi would often times drill a hole through one spot of a door to allow access to the locking mechanism of the door.

The drill could also allow the shinobi to peep inside a location by producing a small and fairly unnoticeable hole, from which the shinobi can observe his target zone. Further still, the shinobi could drill a hole through flame proof material to expose the flammable material underneath. This was common of old Japanese fences and walls. Once a channel to the flammable material was drilled out, the shinobi could insert flammable material down the channel, light it up, and set the structure ablaze.

Smaller drills could also be used to pick the old Japanese locks. Many of the old Japanese padlocks relied on a "prong-and-shell" dynamic. The drill could be inserted through the keyhole and used to manipulate the prongs enough to allow the locking mechanism to slide out of the main casing, this disengaging the lock.

For more information on picking old Japanese locks, one should consult the *Bansenshukai*. Within the final volume of In-Nin, the author presents an extensive amount of information regarding older Japanese locks, the typologies, and the methods for picking them. Specifically, the author mentions the methods for using drills to by-pass locking mechanisms and for altering the keyholes of locks to allow picking.

As such, I will not go into further detail on this matter.

THE SECOND SCROLL

The second scroll changes pace slightly. Whereas the first scroll dealt with more relaxed and detached aspects--- that is, more "unseen shadow" type techniques, the second scroll takes a more active approach.

It opens with Fukushima Ryu methods for shinobi using firearms.

露之印
Mudra of Dew/Tears (Mudra of Mist)

To begin, the main text says:

"Use with muskets."

The Annotations say:

"This is a musket without a bullet. The purpose of this technique is to capture the enemy alive. First, insert gunpowder (down the barrel). Second, insert a considerable amount of ash (instead of a bullet). Being mindful of the timing of the shot, fire this so that the enemy will be blind. Once he is blind, he is vulnerable from the ten directions."

This technique, named "Mudra of Tears" (Dew is a poetic word for tears) is more properly named "Mudra of Mist". This technique is found in Kusunoki Ryu and in Iga Ryu as well. We hold that the origin of this technique is Kusunoki Ryu, from which it this "Mudra of Mist" is found deployed on large scale deployments as well.

In the standard Iga Ryu technique, presented in documents coming a hundred years after the root text was written, the ash/pepper powder is kept in a bamboo tube and dispersed by hand. That version of the technique, found in manuals written much later than the Fukushima manual, is an over simplified version of the original technique.

In Fukushima Ryu's Mudra of Tears, the ash/pepper is turned into a bullet. That is, it becomes a load in the musket and is shot at the person the shinobi wants to take prisoner. Kusunoki Ryu originally did not contain any material involving firearms, as it was made and formulated in the mid 1300s. However, as the tradition was passed down through the years, each generation added additional technique and lore to the tradition. In the mid-1500s, it seems that Kusunoki Masatora added fire arm techniques to the Kusunoki Ryu. One of these techniques was the "Mudra of Mist". In this technique, small cannons and muskets were loaded with the "pepper" and shot into enemy ranks, blinding them in a cloud of eye irritating ash and pepper mixtures. Such a move would either allow your force to escape OR it could be the beginning of an ambush attack. Kusunoki Fuden and Yui Shosetsu also taught the Mudra of Mist technique during the 1600s. It appears in Yui Shosetsu's writings in the "group-usage" form.

Thus, we can see a technique which showcases the relationship between Kusunoki Ryu and Fukushima Ryu, as both traditions utilize firearms to disperse the ash/pepper. Both ryu teach the dual purpose of ambush and/or escape. The Iga manuals tend to be vague on the usage, and considering that the Iga manuals which discuss the Mudra of Mist were written after the Fukushima Ryu manual, we can speculate that the technique may have originated from the Kawachi/Owari families (such as Kusunoki, Yasumi, and Nojiri) and was later adopted by Iga Ryu participants. We know the Nojiri used the technique in Fukushima Ryu. We know that the Kusunoki Ryu contained the technique. We know that the Nojiri and Yasumi families were very closely related, and that Yasumi Ryu Hojutsu (gunnery) was founded in the 1600s. We know that this technique became widely dispersed when Kusunoki Fuden and Yui Shosetsu taught it at the Kusunoki Ryu Gungaku. We know that Iga manuals showcasing this technique were written half-a-century after this. The trail is clear.

It is also important to realize that all of the families involved in the technique are Southern Court loyalists. This provides us with grounds to theorize that the Mudra of Mist/Tears originated as a Go-Nancho technique.

Thus, while it is possible the technique began in Iga and was imported to the Southern Court Loyalist families at a later date, the evidence heavily favors that the technique was developed by the Loyalists and adopted by Iga at a later date.

Let us also not forget that the Southern Court Loyalists have had an on-going guerilla war since the mid-1300s. The Loyalists were assassinating shoguns in the 1400s, before Iga ninjutsu was even conceived.

As the Annotations say, *"Once he is blind, he is vulnerable to the ten directions."*

This is used for capturing hostages. Once they are captured, all of the techniques for what to do with a hostage take place. However, this material was not written down in the main text.

In the present day tradition, shotguns loaded with Pepper/Mace loads are used. While not shot of out muskets, the effect produced is the same in essence.

門破

The Gate Breaker

The main text says:

"This uses three bullets."

The annotations say:

"Place the bullets and insert a fuse through the three bullets. Position the gunpowder between the bullets. Securely wrap the cylinder and secure the outside with ring, similar to the construction of a bucket. When in a position close to the enemy, use the hinawa to ignite each section from behind, going through each part so that each bullet is expelled with a blast, one by one. This is also called 'sequenced musket bullets'."

This is an extension of the intention of Fukushima Ryu's attitude to using firearms. Many Nojiri were expert bowmen, but with the introduction of the firearm and its quick spread among retainers of the Oda/Toyotomi clans, many Nojiri developed a liking for the musket. As previously stated, the Yasumi family developed their own gunnery school in the mid-1600s, Yasumi Ryu Hojutsu. Prior to the formation of the formal school, the techniques existed and were passed through the various branches of the family.

Nojiri Narimasa displays these examples to help remind the student of all the various uses of the musket. Again, like modern day shotgun, there exists a seemingly endless array of shot combinations. In a modern setting, an aspirant to Fukushima Ryu would be expected to study and master and least 5 different loads. The student would not simply learn when to use the load, but they would also learn how to construct the loads.

This highlights a very important aspect of not only Fukushima Ryu, but of the Nojiri/Yasumi teachings. That is:

Guns not being used for shooting people, but rather, guns used as tools (pepper clouds, poison clouds, door breakers, etc.).

In this case, the text explains the idea of producing a multi-shot musket (or a small cannon). While this may not seem very impressive in modern times, this was ground-breaking for the late 1500s. Consider that, while the multi-shot can be used for shooting at another human, the multi-shot can also be used to demolish structures. In particular, it can be used for breaching entry points and creating egress points. The usage of guns against structures (door breaching or setting fires with muskets) is where we see a multitasking effort which exemplifies the spirit of these ninshi.

One should remember that the sequenced shots can be of different loads. For example, you could shoot two breaching rounds to blow open a hole in a wall. Then, shoot a pepper round to blind the inhabitants of the room on the other side of that wall.

In modern times, one understands that multi-shot applies beyond just the rapid succession of shots. In modern context, "multi-shot' – or rather, as a more accurate reading of the kanji would suggests— "sequenced shot", means being able to fire one special round, and then follow it up with a different round. For example, being able to use Door Breaching rounds to get through a barricade, and then quickly load and discharge the Pepper Round. Following that, one quickly loads a bean-bag round.

This idea of keeping a sequence of rounds at a fast pace is the modern meaning of the "multi-shot"/"sequence round".

The Annotations explanation seems to suggest that one could use a musket OR create a similar type of device, constructing it from bamboo. During the Edo period, many of the firearm techniques were changed over from muskets to bamboo tube devices. Just like with the Mudra of Mist, which has a bamboo-tube version (which appeared during the Edo period), we can see that a bamboo-tube version of the Gate Breaker may have existed as well. This would make perfect sense, considering the dynamics of the Edo period.

城工入事
Infiltrating Castles

The root text says:

"

- *Crossing steep areas*
- *Concerning spiked fences*
- *Moving into the horse stables*

There is oral tradition on the above points."

These three points may seem simple enough, but they are a summary of three great principles.

1.) The first point expresses the need to come in from odd locations. It will not do to try and sneak in at well guarded entrances/exits. The shinobi needs to be prepared for complicated and challenging approaches. Even special footwear and tools maybe needed— not for the job inside the castle, but to simply get to the infiltration point !

2.) The second point expresses the need to enter where the people are not looking. Rather than just trying to sneak in through shadows or after an attempt to cleverly evade the watchful eyes of guards, Nojiri is saying that you should enter where they really are not looking. That means a place they have secured and do not believe you will enter from. The example is "over a wall with spikes already in place to keep shinobi out." Guards will not watch a location that seems stupid for the shinobi to enter from. However, if such a spot exist, this is the location you should enter from. Why? Simply put, it is because that location is where the enemy **has a gap in their attention**. It may be difficult to physically get through it, but it is where nobody is actually looking. Rely on the training and the tools, and take advantage of the gap. This principle extends to the psychological "gaps" when referring to undercover infiltrations (false identities, etc.).

3.) The horse stables were a common place for shinobi to operate out of while infiltrating the castle. Old samurai horse stables were similar to western barns in their essence, and as such, provided good cover and space for the shinobi to rest, discuss the assignment, and set up their gear. Also, if capturing hostages, the shinobi could take the first hostage and hide them in the horse stable while they continued any further objectives. The point to make clear is that the horse stables were a very useful "island of fortune" within the enemy compound. The principle presented here is: *"Once inside, find a location that offers space and cover to serve as your base of operations."* This, as stated, would be a place where gear can be arranged, prepared, dismantled, etc. Also, in the old days, if need be, the shinobi could release the horses from the stable if he needed to create a distraction.

In the modern day equivalent, the shinobi would need to find a location, in the enemy territory, to operate from that could also provide some sort of tactical effect to assist the shinobi's exit. One possible modern day example would be a free-standing garage. The agent would sneak onto the property and slip into the garage. Once inside, they prepare for the next phase of their assignment. Once that phase is complete, they retreat back into the garage. Suddenly, an alarm is sounded. The agent needs a fast getaway, so he hotwires a car and make his escape. Again, this teaching emphasizes using some part of the enemy terrain as your base of operations.

The Annotations say:

"This is infiltrating an enemy castle. Enter through trash systems. Cross over the defensive spikes if you intend to cross over a wall. The point is to take advantage of these places. When inside a castle, move into the horse stable. With this, you can know if the horses have been prepared. This will provide you with immediate knowledge of any night raids about to commence. When in a stable, stay behind mounds of grass or straw. Utilizing such locations is a teaching which is key to this transmission of tradition."

This brings up another important point. If the shinobi finds that the horses are not present in the stables or that they are prepared for a night raid, the shinobi would then need to determine if he needs to abandon the mission and make an emergency report to his lord (to wan of the night raid about to take place). One might consider that, after having warned the lord of the night raid, the shinobi may then slip into the enemy rank during the retreat from the night raid. (This is shifting from Innin to Yonin, based on need.)

Let us not forget that, in the beginning, the espionage and covert ops divisions of the samurai army were far more divided. The overly defined word "Shinobi" really came into usage at the end of the 1400s. Prior to the 1400s, several different words were used to describe several different roles. These terms and roles would become muddied in the 1500s, leading to the usage of "shinobi" as a general catch-all term used to describe a vast assortment of tasks.

One of those main tasks has always been, even from the beginning, to slip into the enemy forces at the end of a battle. An extreme amount of effort was put into passwords, codes, signs, etc. to prevent enemy agents from blending in among the ranks during such times. Thus, it is said that after the shinobi warns his lord of the night raid, that he might be able to slip into the enemy ranks afterwards.

Also, if an older and more skilled shinobi is already among the enemy ranks, he can assist the lesser skills shinobi when they successfully blend into the general population.

This allows us the moment to ponder the reality that, even when innin shinobi was sneaking in under the cover of darkness, the Yonin shinobi are already present among the enemy ranks. It is important to never forget that you need both Yonin undercover agents and Innin infiltrators. Expert shinobi would be able to shift between the two functions as needed.

源氏入黒
The House of Genji's Ink Stick ("Tattoo" in the Annotations)

The main text says:

"Use the oil of namomi (Japanese cocklebur)"

The annotations further explain with :

"Take oil of cocklebur and apply it onto a staff or similar pieces of wood (canes, etc.) so that when you strike with the wood, it will break through anything."

Namomi refers to the East Asian Cocklebur, not to be confused with the North American Cocklebur, introduced to Japan in 1928 and now considered an invasive species. There is also another plant, which has a very distinct five pronged blossom, which also carries the name "namomi" when referring to the leaves specifically.

Interestingly enough, "namomi" is the name of a skin rash caused by too much time spent around fire hearths. There is a type of demon associated with this condition, called "namahage", which is connected to stories of rooster calls and rescuing captive women (both of which have significance within this tradition). Although, the similarities are only a coincidence, I thought it would be fun to mention it.

This technique is, essentially, a battering ram. The oil makes the wood extremely durable. The oiled wooden stick is the "tattoo" because it, like a tattoo, the ink (the oil) has been put inside the wood (like ink into the skin). "Ink Stick" is self explanatory. As stated, this tool is used to batter doors, fences, windows, etc.

If need be, this tool could be used as a weapon. However, its primary function is to batter barricades. That is, the primary function of this device in Fukushima Ryu is for it to be used as a battering ram.

The technique was formulated and handed down from the House of Genji, of which several samurai families descend.

As previously said, it should be noted that the Kusunoki Ryu is based on Genji traditions mixed with Chinese Warfare and Esoteric Buddhism. Also, the Nojiri trace back to Genji Yorimitsu. Thus, the inclusion of the Genji battering ram is as poetic as it is logical.

矢打留様
Stopping Arrows

The main text says:

"This is used for stopping arrows."

The Annotations say:

"This is accomplished by using a large wheel made of bamboo, similar to the wheel of a pulling cart. Put a hole at the hub and insert a pole. Rotate the wheel so that arrows will be stopped."

This technique may seem unbelievable to some readers. Consider that this technique has been recorded in many battles outside of Japan. This technique was even recorded in some ancient Greco-Roman wars, in which the wheels were made of stone and spun atop the fortress walls. It is actual history. These stone wheels allowed the defenders to see out, but be protected from incoming projectiles. The stone wheels are recorded to have worked to an excellent degree.

Consider that, when this manual was written, Japan did not have any material to provide them with an option to both view and defend. That is, when a wave of arrows were shot, the only defense was to "turtle up" behind something thick and impenetrable. This, however, came at the cost of not being able to see.

This technique is a progressive and clever approach to allowing defense and visibility. That is the exact "feeling" that I advise the reader to take away from this technique. Combiming this technique with the boat (which appears later) is a form of a Kusunoki Ryu technique called "Escape from Certain Death".

咽乾ヌ薬
Cotton Mouth Pills

These pills are for when you have cotton-mouth (dry mouth and dry throat). Cotton Mouth can have a dramatic impact on your ability to focus and function, and is usually the result of various reactions in your body (nervousness being one such source for cotton mouth). Also, some people, when not telling the truth, may develop cotton mouth. It can also be due to a lack of hydration. The sources of cotton mouth are many. When you have cotton mouth, take the pills.

It should be noted that this is not meant to cure Xerostomia, but rather, this is used to stave off thirst and reduce the effect of temporary cotton mouth symptoms (due to nervousness, etc).

The main text says :

"

- *Unripe green plum*
- *Toboshi*

Powder equal amounts of the above and make pills the size of soy beans. Take one pill with water"

The Annotations say :

" Toboshi is 'taito mochi' rice in the husk. You should take a pill every morning. It is also advisable to take a pill before you go into combat."

The reader may find the phrase *"take with water"* to be odd. However, if the reader has ever suffered cotton-mouth, they would do well to remember that a drink of water is insufficient to cure the cotton-mouth. Therefore, taking the pill with a little water is nothing odd.

This can, in a pinch, be used to reserve your water supply. In this case, you do not have cotton-mouth, but you use the pills to stave off any thirst. This helps to maintain your water supply if you, for whatever reason, are in a situation where you need to preserve your water.

中ノ大 迯術
Middle-High Escape Art

This next technique is related to escaping. It may seem simple, but the roots of this spell are profound and it should not be taken lightly.

The main text says:

"Face the direction you will travel and bow three times.

Chant : 武士ノ腰ニ差タル鍔刀事ノツマツキアラセ給ナ"

The Annotations say :

" "Cut the kuji to the right and the left."

The critical point of this is the combination of the actual spell with the simple directive of intention and reliance on faith. As you will see later, the Fukushima Ryu practitioner places a considerable amount of the loyalty to their sense of Faith and Intuition.

Here is the spell as it appears in the main manual:

文ニ曰武士ノ腰ニ差タル鍔刀事ノツマヅキアラゼ給ヒ

Note:

As for "cutting to the right and left", it is the Nine Slash grid. As we know, this is the symbol of Doman and is used to expel negative forces. Therefore, cutting to the right and left is simply to expel negative/vengeful ghosts from your path.

When translated into English, the spell roughly means *"As a bushi, may I have no mishaps with my katana or its pieces while on my journey."* In modern times, you could ideally substitute any weapon or piece of equipment. For example, you could say *"As a private detective, may I have no mishaps with any of my gear or any of my gear's parts during my investigation"* or you could say *"As a soldier, may I have no mishaps with my rifle, or any of the parts of my rifle, while deployed."* Albeit, there is a magical origin to the original poem, so there is still value in expressing the original poem even in modern times. It is important to note that the weapon or gear is an effigy for the operation. The focus on the entire weapon and the parts of the weapon is an effigy for the fact that an operation is not a single "thing", but a composite of smaller parts. Therefore, we ask to have no malfunction with the entire object nor any of the constituent parts.

Also, when cutting the Nine Slash grid, one can use whichever variation of the Kuji Kiri they wish. For example, one can use the original Taoist system or one of the Esoteric Pure Land versions. I personally prefer the Esoteric Pure Land versions.

人ノ宅 エ入事
The Matter of Entering People's Houses

The main text says:

"Remove the eyes of a dog, be it still alive or dead. Then string the eyes on the hair from a horse's tail. Apply a layer of liquid gold. Next, apply lacquer and dry in the shade for 100 days. Carry this in a crimson bag. There are oral traditions."

The Annotations say:

"This is the manner by which shinobi-no-hito can protect themselves from being detected other people. Proceed with the crimson bag attached to your forehead. This will allow you to clearly see your enemies while the enemies cannot see you."

This is a Fukushima Ryu spell used to make the wearer of the amulet invisible to guards, and in particular, to dogs. There is also a version of the spell found in later Iga Ryu manuals, which is a little different. The eyes of the dog are ripped out, dried, and placed in a red cloth, which is then folded and kept on the shinobi. In this version, the eyes of the dog are ties by horse hair, and gold leaf/liquid gold and lacquer are applied. Instead of a red cloth, the amulet is kept inside of a crimson bag. This bag is then kept, similar to a "medicine pouch", by the shinobi and invoked during the field operations.

Again, this is related to dog magic. Many people did cruel things to dogs in order to have quick access to a potent magical source. However, such cruelty is not without steep cost. Therefore, many alternatives exist to some of the more brutal forms of the magic. In times of war, mutilating a dog was not something looked down upon. The Sengoku period was truly a hellish place. When a man spent his life ending the lives of other men, torturing and killing a dog was not something of an odd sort at all. However, in more civilized and peaceful times, when the chance to enact a more virtuous set of behaviors is possible, we should strive to use the less horrific methods and versions of the spells. Therefore, as previously mentioned, the shinobi should use the eyes of a recently deceased dog. Also, the shinobi should not torture and mutilate a dog for special access to a vengeful ghost. Simply use the Inu-Gami (paper dog) version of the spell to secure the helper. There are also further dog magic spells, such as one that uses the dogs tail. However, this tail can be taken from a dead dog. It does not have to be ripped or chopped from a living dog. The idea is that the torment of the animal charged the energy traces (residual energy) and, even though of a traumatic nature, these traces empowered the body part dramatically. I say that such brutality is not required and, while the brutal methods are here-in explained for their historical and cultural value, I greatly push and support the less horrific variations.

In Fukushima Ryu, you can use the eyes of a dead dog. There is no need to be cruel. There is also a way to cross this spell with the Inu-Gami spell.

One can become invisible to the enemy by three means:

1.) **Interdependent conditions:** This is when there is no spirits or Siddhis or blessings. Simply, you bring together items with the proper meaning/energy to perform a task. For example, pit viper fangs in your top knot can help make you disappear from your enemy. This is a natural power of the fangs.

2.) **Intervention of Worldly Gods and/or Spirits**: This is when you perform a specific spell that involves a worldly god and/or spirits, and then you are hidden from your enemies as a result of this arrangement. This is like when you make spells for spirits or gods to bless you with invisibility.

3.) **Siddhis and Blessings:** This is when you have the blessing of an Enlightened Being or you have attained a high level of realization. Your invisibility is the result of your ability to bend the mundane world or you have the blessings of Enlightened Beings and Dharma Protectors.

The Dog-Eye Magic is related to Dog magic, which is a mixture of Type 1 and Type 2 from the list above. It is type one because it relies on the natural energy/meaning of the Dog, but when you involve any form of invocation of a deceased dog (a Dog spirit), this becomes the second type of invisibility.

Lastly, the crimson bag is not tied to the forehead by itself. Ideally, the crimson pouch is folded into a crimson headband and the headband is worn around the head. In actuality, you don't see the bag. I should also note that this bag is a talisman bag, and as such, is fairly small and flat. It folds into the headband.

綱朽之事
Decaying/Ruining Rope

The root text says:

" *Mica*
Mercury
Oil of ray fish

Apply this mixture to rope and the rope will immediately decay. There are oral traditions for this. "

The Annotations say:

"This is a substance that causes rope to decay and waste away. The ingredients are mica and oil of the ray fish."

There are numerous purposes for this technique, so its specific usage is not limited to any one point in time. Ideally, we can imagine a Fukushima Ryu shinobi sneaking into a location and covertly rubbing the mixture on support lines, then retreating. Without any indication or warning, those support lines would become compromised. It would allow a delay between the act of sabotaging the lines and the actual breaking of the lines.

Furthermore, it could be used to compromise suspension lines on things like suspension ladders and bridges. When a shinobi is forced to leave a rope hanging, he can put this substance on the rope in order to cause the rope to decay.

This can also be used to ambush or assassinate targets, by compromising the suspension lines of various devices, such as boats and bridges.

夜物ノ躰ヲ知事
Knowledge of Nighttime Forms

The root text says:

" *Chant:* ヒトフタミヨイツムユナ丶ヤコ丶ノタリモ丶チヨロ

Chant three times and then put both hands together. There is an additional action that needs to be done at this point. Next, move your hands into "diamond position" and observe what is present by looking (through the diamond)."

The Annotations says:

"The action of 'putting your hands together' means to use 'gassho' (hands together in prayer). Then, open and spread your palms to make a diamond shape. If you look through this gap, then your mental fetters will calm down and you will be settled. When a person is calm and focused, proper understanding will manifest. This leads to better judgments. Chant the poem three times"

This is not meant to convey divine eye. That is, this is not meant to allow you to see spirits or ghouls. This is a technique to, essentially, calm your mind and focus your night vision so that you can correctly see mundane objects at night. Night time navigation is not something one can do as a novice, especially in the olden times. Anyone who has ever spent a night in the woods, far away from street lights and cell phone signals, knows how easy one can become lost. Even in villages, towns, etc... night time movement can be difficult because, at night, one's eyes constantly adapt and shift to various and ever-changing levels of light. Shadow-like illusions move and shift in one's vision, giving the feeling that there is movement where there is none. The contour of objects seems to shift and change in the darkness. A shinobi needs to have a mind that is capable of clearly seeing landmarks and individuals at night, while keeping a mental map of the landscape and its inhabitants. This technique helps to calm the visual tricks and relax the mind.

If someone has divine eye through other methods, then this would allow them to calm down and focus, but the power would exist prior to this method. There are many spells which will allow someone to see ghosts and ghouls. Many of the spells involve paper-spells which must be empowered, chanted, burned to ash, and the ashes then drunk and rubbed on the eyes. However, I must caution the reader that such spells provide no protection from ghost and ghouls. In fact, once a ghost realizes that you can see it, it may begin to haunt you and demand you to take action on its behalf. Therefore, I highly advise the readers to avoid trying to see ghosts and ghouls. It is not a game.

太刀落ス之事
The Matter of Knocking Down A Sword

The root text says:

- *Collect thirty three 'Dairyo' spiders and put them in a cylinder until they die*
- *The blood of a newt*
- *Fruit of the honeysuckle*

Mix these ingredients together (and spread the mixture on your hands). Your hands will not get cut. This is also referred to as "Receiving a Blade with the Hands".

The Annotations state:

"The fruit of the honeysuckle is an ingredient used in medicine and can also be called toronashi."

Tachi Otoshi (knocking down/falling a sword) is a well-known technique in many martial arts systems. This technique is named after that technique, but this Fukushima Ryu technique is NOT the same technique. **This is not a martial art technique, it is a magical technique.**

In this Fukushima Ryu technique, the hands are made invulnerable to cuts due to the magical mixture. This allows the Fukushima Ryu

74

shinobi to, rather than use something like a bo (staff) to disarm a sword, use his bare hands to disarm an attacker.

I also take this opportunity to remind the reader that there is a third Fukushima Ryu manual (of which the full content is not included in this book) which further discusses the "spider hands" technique. I discussed this aspect in *IN PRAISE OF SPIES (2012)*. Beyond making your hands invulnerable to cuts, this magical mixture also causes your hands to be more nimble and "sticky". The shinobi will not drop his sword during a fight, nor any of his tools (such as lock picking tools).

Also, it should be mentioned that the honeysuckle mentioned in this text is, as should be obvious, the Japanese version of the Honeysuckle. It is a vine-like shrub which has many medicinal uses. The leaves can be used as a poultice for everything from skin rashes to helping with bronchial issues. The leaves of the plant can be briefly heated over a candle flame and placed on the forehead to help with headaches.

The fruit, a small firm black berry containing many seeds, can be eaten raw to help with headaches and fevers. The seeds of the fruit are often used, dried, as a component in de-worming medication. The fruit and seeds can be powdered and used on open wounds to prevent infection. Diffusing the fruit and seeds into an oil can be used to treat some topical parasites.

鬼卜見スル術
Art of Arising as a Demon

The root text states:

"

- *Capture fireflies and toads on the seventh day of the seventh month*
- *On the fifth day of the fifth month, extract 'oil of the rat' and harvest the liver of bats.*

Make pills of this mixture and eat the pills. You will arise as a demon for one night. "

The Annotations say: *"This is a way to help your mind avoid cowardice."*

The seventh day of the seventh month is Tanabata Night, also known as the Star Festival. On this night, the deities Orihime and Hikoboshi (deities associated with particular star constellations) are allowed to come together. The rest of the year, the Milky Way forbids them to see each other. This night is also a special time where Shinto shrine maidens performed rituals and prayers by rivers for good harvests in the coming autumn.

This is the night to collect fireflies. This is also important because the fireflies are frequently found to hover around river banks (where the Shinto rituals for good autumn will be taking place). The fireflies represent the passion between lovers (reflecting Tanabata Night). But, beyond that, the fireflies represent the spirits of the dead, in particular, the spirits of dead warriors. These dead warriors speak to the living by the language of the flashing lights of the fireflies. Furthermore, they speak to the living out of their love and duty to the living.

The toad is also a magically potent animal throughout Japanese folklore. Appearing in many stories, toads are considered to be symbols of 'wisdom earned from traveling" and longevity. It is also said that the Shinto deity Kuyebiko (the Scarecrow god) used toads as his messengers. Kuyebiko is believed to be aware of all the movements of heaven and earth, and can be summoned for divination purposes.

Furthermore, there is a Taoist legend of a man named Bagen. Bagen followed the Taoist deity Gama Sennin to a river one evening. At the river, Gama Senin gave Bagen a magical pill which turned him into a toad demon. From this toad demon, a "division" of toad demons came into being. If these toad demons are found and consulted, they can teach human beings magical arts. In particular, the toad demons teach the arts of transforming shape and appearance.

It is this conflux of energy (stars, love, duty, deceased warriors, longevity, wisdom, and transformation) that the spells captures when it uses the fireflies and toads. The toad represents the ability to shift into a demon, and the fireflies represent the energetic fuel (love, war, duty) which provides color to the experience.

The fifth day of the fifth month is when the sun is considered to be strongest. This is known as the "Dragon Boat Festival Day". This day is a celebration of Naga (dragons). Naga/dragons are giant horned serpents that maintain their kingdoms in the oceans and waters of the world. On this day, offerings can be dumped into rivers for the nagas.

There is also a history regarding the Chinese kingdom of Wu. It is said that the ruler, named Fuchai, was ignorant. There was a brilliant strategist and spy-master named Wu Zixu. Fuchai, in his envy and ignorance, forced Wu Zixu to commit suicide on this day. Wu Zixu's body was then dumped into a river. It is believed that the killing and dumping of Wu Zixu's body into the river was a dishonorable act, an insult to the Naga king. This action brought great misfortune to the kingdom of Wu.

Thus, on this day, gather the correct ingredients. Eating these pills will cause one to arise as a demon for the course of a night.

Since these pills can only be made once a year, the Fukushima Ryu shinobi would make many pills each time. That is, one does not make a single pill each year. One makes a supply of pills for the entire year.

The liver of the bat actually affects one's chi and improves night vision.

Of course, there is more to this pill than even written in this commentary.

太刀燃ル術
Art of Igniting the Sword ("Burning sword")

The root text says:

"Mix namomi into oil and mix. Coat the blade"

The Annotations further state:

"This technique involves applying a substance to your sword. When facing the enemy, they see your burning sword. The purpose of this is to seize the enemy's chi. This oil is made from cocklebur."

So, is this sword a burning sword? Yes. But, what do we mean by burning?

Do we mean that the sword is literally set on fire? Let us examine a few factors. The Annotations say that the sword will steal the chi of the enemy. As we will go over several times in this text, chi has a three layer meaning. However, starting with the most fundamental layer (chi = attention), we can see that a burning sword would cause the enemy to lose attention. First, the elemental quality of fire is to pull attention. Secondly, while the flames of the sword are easy to see, the actual blade becomes very difficult to see. The blade disappears into a conflagration streaking through space. So, is it possible that the text speaks of setting your sword on fire to keep your enemy from being able to focus on your blade? Does the fire of the sword disrupt the energy flow of the conflict, absorbing some element of the enemy's attention on an energetic level?

What if the sword is not actually on fire? What if the oil, mixed on the blade, doesn't physically ignite the blade, but "ignites" it in an energetic way? What if the combination of the metal and the oil ignites the elemental quality of the blade? What if that quality has the ability to steal chi?

Rather than telling you the answer, I suggest that the reader should look into this topic on their own. Of course, I am not responsible for what may come from such experimentation. Playing with flaming swords is extremely dangerous.

門出之大事
The Great Matter of Exiting Through Gates

The root text says:
"Whether it be the direction of the Ox, the Ram, the Dog, or the Dragon... all directions are protected by the gods, and therefore it is not proper to shun any direction." [see below concerning translation]
Chant the above three times.

Next, draw the kanji 勝 *(victory) in your left palm three times with your right finger and then close your left hand into a fist. After (having gone through the gate) and traveled two or three ken from the gate, then open your palm and recite:*

"We attach cotton shide to the tamagushi (a shinto wand made of shide and sakaki tree branch) and we commit to the Buddha and the Tao. No mist blocks our path."

Chant the above three times.

There is a significant amount of kuden."

The Annotations say:

"The key is to not look behind you until you have ventured two or three measures past the gate. At that point, open your closed fist and lick your palm."

The first poem approximately translates to: *"Whether it be the direction of the Ox, the Ram, the Dog, or the Dragon... all directions are protected by the gods, and therefore it is not proper to shun any direction."*

The original poem is in poetic form and is difficult to translate directly, as it requires a considerable amount of commentary to clear up a portion of the spell. As such, I have chosen to simply include an appropriate approximation of the verse. The intention and meaning remains the same.

Roughly said, the verse is to remind the shinobi that divine protection exists in all directions at all times. The shinobi should not worry about any interfering ghosts or demons at this time.

There are two other spells from the Owari area (where this spell came from) that are used to ward off evil spirits and are similar to the original spells listed in the manual. The first is used to ward off ill-omens, and translates approximately to *"May the winds from Ise Shrine quickly blow through this place."*

The other spell, more directly related to this spell, approximately means: *"Big or small, if it is not the child of a kami, may it not be allowed to pass through here."*

The feeling of this second spell (and some of the wording of the original spell in Japanese) is more accurate to the actual spell listed in the manual. **You could also say the original spell in the manual means something similar to**: *"No matter what direction or time, only the children of kami are allowed to pass through this gate."*

Again, while not directly translating the spell, the "feeling" and meaning are intact.

After getting through the gate and making it about 30 paces away, you should open your hand and recite the second poem. Again, the original poem is difficult to translate directly and I have chosen to present an approximation of the meaning. The poem refers to using a tamagushi (Shinto wand made of cotton strips attached to sakaki branch) to brush and purify the spell away. This is a method to clear the spell off of the caster and leave the entire situation behind.

As the author, I apologize for not going with the original poems, but they contain some wording and meaning which would undoubtedly be misconstrued outside of a significant amount of research and understanding. To avoid this confusion, as stated, I have provided approximation of equivalent meaning.

My approximations, and the attempts to convey the "feeling", could be construed as an aspect of the kuden.

The Annotations contain an interesting shift or possible error. The original spell calls for the shinobi to blow the spell off his hand. The Annotations appear to call for the shinobi to lick his hand, which is different that the original spell. This shift from blowing to licking either came about due to deliberate change in the spell (in Terasawa Sensei's lineage) or a flat out mistake.

It is also taught that, when writing the kanji on your left hand, you should consider your finger to be a willow brush infused with the power of Ise Shrine (like in the dream spell).

When blowing the spell off of your hand, you are to envision that your breath is like the cotton white shide dusting the spell off of your hand, putting an end to the spell. You need to remember your devotion to the Buddhas and the Tao in order to finalize the purification.

You can also write the seed syllable for Amida Buddha or the syllable "A" in your hand and chant the nembutsu or one of the esoteric nembustu as well. In that case, when you open your hand, imagine the syllable merges with space.

秘極之薬之事
Most Secret Medicine

The root text says:
"

- *Soak a large amount of (Japanese) Sweetflag root in sake*
- *Gather a medium amount of the peel of a Satsuma*
- *Soak a medium amount of Japanese Tallow in water*
- *A medium amount of fire roasted ginseng*

Powder these ingredients. Make pills.

If you drink alcohol then make pills by using sake. If you abstain from alcohol, then by using tea or water, as well as during times of war, make the pills by using rice broth.

The above medicine is used in battle or any important situation. This it works for all sicknesses, especially as a stimulant."

There is not much to be said other than to discuss the ingredients. I will attempt to go over each ingredient in order.

1.) Sweetflag: By itself, it can be soaked in water, rice broth, or alcohol. However, I have heard reports that soaking it in alcohol makes it taste terrible. As I do not drink alcohol, I have never done this, so I cannot confirm or deny this claim. However, for this medicine, the shinobi will powder the sweetflag after it has been soaked. This powder alone can serve as a medicine for ailments such as most issues involving stomach sickness. Examples would be nausea, heartburn, and stomach inflammation.
The ROOT of the Sweetflag can be soaked and powdered as well. The root is more suited to fight colds and infections, etc.

2.) The peel of the Satsuma will give the medicine the flavor of the Satsuma, because the powders taste bad. There is –some- health benefit from the peel, but it is mostly for taste to be honest.

3.) Japanese Tallow can make you sick on its own, so it must be soaked and powdered. Generally speaking, it is a purge ingredient and should be treated with caution. Too much Tallow can make one very violently ill.

4.) The Japanese Ginseng is actually a weaker version of the North American and/or Chinese species. This ginseng should be fire roasted before being powdered. Also, I should point out that there is a big misconception regarding Ginseng in the modern world. Ginseng is not a "hot" ingredient. Ginseng is classified as "sweet" and "small cold". It is actually not meant to be used to speed the flow of Chi, that job belongs to Ginger (as will be addressed later in the commentary). Ginseng helps address issues of the spleen, the kidney, the heart, and lungs (all five). As a "sweet", it gives extra attention to the spleen and to calming irritation. As a "minor cold", it specifically calms the energy flow. This specifically addresses stress reduction.

This pill is very balanced and will help keep oneself healthy and relaxed.

SCROLL 3

息ノキレヌ薬 人

The root text says: *"Medicine for breathing issues – person"*

The Annotations says: *"Rub 'oil of human' or 'oil of toad' onto your lips. You can also just hold toad skin in your mouth."*

This is to calm issues related to allergies and asthma. "Oil of human" is actually horse fat. Spread it on your lips like lip balm and breathe in the vapors.

夜物音ヲ聞事 風

The root text says: *"Listening to the sounds of the things at night – wind"*

The Annotations says: *"Crouch and listen on the downside side. Hearing from upwind is difficult."*

This is pure physics. Sound waves carry on the wind. Thus, the sound waves do not travel against the wind. Upwind is a poor position. The enemy can hear and smell anything you do, while you cannot smell or hear them. If you have to make noise, make the noise when the when is going away from the enemy, so that the sound will travel on the air away from the enemy.

忍入時之事 八

The root texts says: *"Times to infiltrate – eight"*

The Annotations say: *"Infiltrate during the eighth portion of the night. This is when people will be deeply asleep. During the day, the eighth portion is when most people serve meals and this time period is a "gap" (虚), which is ideal for infiltration. Furthermore, you should infiltrate during the hour of the year that the enemy commander was born. The hour of the sign in which year the commander was born is also a "gap". For example, if the enemy commander was born in the Year of the Rat, then infiltrate at the hour of the Rat."*

The kanji "虚" appears numerous times in the text. On one hand, it means "insubstantial" or "void". On the other hand, it means "crack" or "empty space". Both meanings apply, and "虚" becomes something equivalent to "間". In ninjutsu, these terms have a dual meaning. First, they refer to a physical gap in the attention of the enemy. Secondly, and more profoundly, they refer to the insubstantial aspects of the enemy. The insubstantial aspect is the formless aspect of the enemy, such as his chi, his emotions, his thoughts, and his spiritual patterns and habituations. The shinobi specializes in sneaking through physical "gaps" and sneaking into the "gaps" of the enemy's life. The shinobi is both an infiltrator of the physical landscape and the mental landscape.
In this particular case, there is a relationship between the year the enemy commander is born and the "gaps" which appear during the hours of the day and night.

However, it needs to be stressed that the root text advises to enter during the eight portion. It is Terasawa Sensei who suggests entering in regards to the Year/Hour relationship. These are two distinct techniques and the reader needs to remember that Nojiri, in the original text, is essentially gives a standard time to enter. The Annotations give a method for determining this time, which can change based on the factors.

While these two methods to not always contradict, they may sometimes contradict. Therefore, one needs to remember who is saying what and choose the method they will rely on.

敵之心騒セ申事 － 夢

The root text says: *"Disturbing the Enemy's Mind – Dreams"*

The Annotations say: *"This means to cause the enemy commander to dream of obstacles. You can write that a specific retainer of the enemy commander is colluding against him, and it will appear this way in the enemy commander's dream."*

This refers to the spell of Interlocking Dreams. When it says *"you can write"*, this refers to adding this function to the paper spell. This method is considered a master level technique among this tradition.

忍ニアハヌ薬 - 生姜

The root text says :

"Medicine to protect from shinobi - Ginger. This can be used for all things."

The Annotations say:

"Grate ginger into a mash and then spread it thinly into a 1 sun square on paper. Use a thin glue to adhere the paper firmly onto your belly button . This medicine prevents sleep. It can be used to work against cold and heat. You should have no doubts about this technique. It is an amazing medicine."

My family still uses this technique. You do just as instructed. Grate ginger into a mash and put it in your belly button. Cover your belly button with a large bandage. You can also put additional ginger mash under your tongue. This will come up again later in the manual.

行燈ノ火カクス事

The root text says: *"Hiding the light of an andon (permanent paper covered oil lantern)."*

The Annotations say: *"Do this in a way that the various kenuki hold the plates in place."*

Andon lanterns were wooden beam lanterns, with paper coverings and oil fed flame on the inside. If one needed to hide this light, they ran the risk of putting the fire and they may not have the means for relighting the lantern. For this, one is instructed to use boards to cover the faces of the lamp and hold these in place with a types of kenuki. Kenuki refers to metal clips. Kenuki can also mean an old japanese "tweezer" tool. In that case, the shinobi would hold the board in place with these tweezers.

In the modern day, preserving the light of the lantern would not be much of a concern, but this technique reminds us of the context of the world the shinobi lived in.

城内又ハ人ニ知ラレヌ書状書様
付タリ見様ノ事

The root text says:

"The types of writing covert documents which are sent into enemy castles and cannot be read by unintended individuals and the various ways of reading the documents"

The Annotations say:

"This technique is for when someone is separated from their allies and need to exchange documents. This entails writing with a mixture with soy bean milk, the liquid used to strain teeth or with the juice of the Yuzu fruit. Reading entails holding the document over a fire or covering the document in water. The liquid used to stain teeth cannot be seen unless the document is covered in water. I want to state that if you use the tooth staining liquid you should put a layer of ink on the backside of the paper. The writing will not absorb the ink and be clearly seen."

This is one of the few places in which the actual espionage techniques of the House of Nojiri make an appearance in this manual (as the majority of the manual are dedicated to the more extravagant tools, spells, and techniques).

Covert communication is a critically important and fundamental skill in any espionage system. This technique is explained in the famous *Bansenshukai* manual.

Soy bean milk and yuzu juice dry clear and can be revealed by covering the paper in water or holding it up to a heat source.

酉
Roosters

The root text says :

"Use 酉 seven times.
Use a toothpick made from the Sakaki tree.
Write it on the pathways that people will use (walk on).
At night, write 酉 on the left and right of your pillow."

The Annotations say:

" 'Seven Roosters' In this text, the 酉 refers to roosters. Regardless of the hour, write 酉 seven times, on each side of your pillow, while praying and requesting to be alerted (startled) at the exact hour you wish. Then, sleep. 酉 is the astrological symbol for Rooster. This is used because the roosters will inform you of the hour. This is a magical ritual."

Also included in the Annotations is another spell:

"通道ノ書" means "Walkway's document". Have a pit viper(mamushi) bite a new ink stone. Then, write with that ink. Anything that you write will come to pass. Do this by capturing a live pit viper. Secure its body and open the viper's mouth. Have the viper bite a new ink stone. Put the ink stone into a pottery jar and close it with a lid. Bury the jar in the ground of a road where people walk, for seven days. Afterwards, dig up the jar and take the ink stone out. Write anything you wish with this ink and your wish will come true."

The first thing that needs to be clarified is that the rooster spirits are a form of shikigami, that is, helper spirits. There is another version of this spell which uses small clay human-shaped dolls, sometimes even paper cut-out dolls, which are placed in key locations. The effigies are then asked to please alert in case any enemies pass by. This is similar to the Inu-Gami spell mentioned earlier. When writing the kanji for Rooster, try to think that you are actually requesting seven distinct rooster spirits to aid you. They have the "feeling" of being scouts.

The Seven Roosters are not a random number. These seven specific Rooster spirits are an actual group of spirits which have been invoked by various priests, sorcerers, etc. throughout Asia. Without digressing too far, we can examine these seven briefly. The most venerated and sacred of the seven is the "White Rooster", considered foremost among the seven. It is associated with chasing away demons and ghosts. This white rooster was venerated in China by Taoist, but when his invocation came to Japan, he became associated with Shinto. The second most well-known rooster, the "Red Rooster", protects from fire and other disasters. The remaining five roosters are associated with various schema of five. That is, you can say they embody "the five constant factors of war" or the "five social virtues". Alternatively, you can consider that each rooster, aside from the five factors, still represents some sort of protection, such as protection from poverty and protection from sickness.

The rooster is also associated with the bringing of Amaterasu forth from her hiding. The rising of the sun, and its subsequent dispelling of darkness, is further tied to the rooster's ability to dispel demons and ghosts. Interestingly enough, the comb of the rooster's crown is associated with a sacred comb given to the rooster by Amaterasu. There is an additional magical spell associated with this. According to tradition, one takes an unused comb and sits facing east, just before sunrise. As the sunrises, invoke the seven roosters and carve or paint "酉" (seven times) on one side. Then, do the same with "伊" on the other side of the comb. When you do this, considering that you are hearing the roosters calling out. Comb your hair with the comb and say *"Please do not forget your promise"*. Then, place the comb in your hair and continue to watch the sunrise. Afterwards, this comb can be wrapped in white cloth, preferably with cedar or sakaki, and put somewhere safe and/or sacred. You can then wear this comb in your hair to dispel any demons or ghost which would assail you on your ventures.

In shinobi arts, many types of items are worn in the hair for magical protection. These range from enchanted combs, hairpins, snake fanges, and Buddhist amulets and miniature statues of Buddhist deities. Specifically, one can also wear small amulets of female

Buddhas (i.e. Marishiten, etc) or Dakini in their hair to also obtain invisibility from demons and ghosts.

The rooster's direction is West (which is why the astrological symbol for rooster looks almost identical to the symbol for west). There is a type of very powerful rooster spirit that is said to appear occasionally. It is said that this spirit requires that the person summoning it must be of extremely high moral fiber and offer forth morning dew as an offering.

Lastly, the rooster represents, among warriors, courage and ferocity.

As for the "Walkway's Document", you have to understand that when it says *'anything you wish for'* is due to the magical quality of the ink you have created. This ink is powerful not because of the ink itself, but because of the types of spirits it will attract. Those spirits will be compelled to answer your prayer/wish far quicker and with much higher efficiency due to the ink you have used. What is NOT mentioned here is the need to actually write a proper paper-spell. You cannot simply write some random desire in English. The assumption of the text is that the reader will know that the spell is referring to the creation of a proper paper-spell.

Thus, if you write your legit paper-spell with this ink, it will become far more potent.

Furthermore, it should be understood that pit vipers have a large amount of spiritual symbolism and power associated with them. As stated, their fangs and venom, when worn in the top knot, can be enough to make you invisible to your enemies. Snakes are guardians of life and death. The snake itself represents various qualities of fertility and life, but their venom shows that they also have the authority and power to issue death. Snakes are also connected to Naga, and as such, are believed to be associated with rain and thunder spirits. Writing with snake venom, as such, gives one more spiritual authority when dealing with spirits.

水練之事
Water Training

The root text says: *"The measurement is 1 shaku 4 sun. There is a considerable amount of oral tradition (kuden) to accompany this device."*

The Annotations say: *"This device is a method to stay submerged for longer periods of time without (having to rise to the surface) to take a breath. Construct this so that it is 1 shaku 4 sun. Make it from leather and coat it in tung oil. Craft a tube of deer horn, similar to the tip of the gunpowder containers used with muskets. This will allow you to keep hold of with your mouth. The tip of this tube is to be made of copper. Fashion the seal out of toad skin to keep water from getting inside. Please a ball of lead in the pouch."*

This device is truly one that requires in-person instruction. Nojiri Narimasa was well aware of the difficulty in explaining and teaching such a device through written text alone. As seen, the root text mentions the dimensions and that kuden is required. As such, the entry is merely a memory aid. The Annotations seek to explain the technique further. However, even with more details revealed, the scope of the device is not transmitted by mere words.

I, therefore, will equally fail in my attempt to explain this device further. Knowing the limitations of written word, I begin by saying that this device is indeed an underwater breathing-bag. The metal ball placed inside is to counter balance the buoyancy of the air within the pouch. The bag is made of leather and coated in tung oil. Tung oil is a type of oil made from pressing the seeds of the Tung tree. This oil dries into a clear and plastic-like finish. This is used to water-proof the bag. In China, tung oil was painted onto the bottom of boats to waterproof the vessels.

The device appears under the heading "Water Training". This is significant. This device is not meant to be used in an isolated manner. Rather, this device is used in conjunction with all the training associated with all aquatic operations. These various operations are not mentioned in the root text or annotations, but I will go over them briefly. The aquatic training covers such things as swimming underwater, free diving, covert entry and exit via water, and emergency situations. In each of these situations, having an air supply which is easily accessible is very useful.

For example, when escaping enemies, one can submerge and either swim or "bottom walk" (as found in free diving) to get away. While submerged, one can (in conjunction with breath training) get additional air from the pouch. This prevents the shinobi from having the breach the surface. This principle applies to entering locations covertly as well. Since water has been, and continues to be, a difficult medium to guard, then water becomes poorly guarded. This makes aquatic insertion and egress ideal. Even in the present day, special operations units make amphibious insertions and extractions. Thus, the mention of this device in the manual is more of a memory aid, serving to remind the Fukushima Ryu shinobi of all the aquatic training they have undergone. Also, in terms of sheer emergencies, the breathing bag can also be used to help a shinobi caught in choppy waters without a boat or a floatation device. The shinobi would seek to breathe air from above the water, but they might be occasionally forced under water for prolonged periods of time by violent waves. Having an air supply, in case of severe emergency, may be the difference between life and death.

The diagram does not explain nor show any cords, but one can tie the bag to one's chest or even strap it around one's fact. The metal ball does counteract the buoyancy, but the bag can still pull to various directions. Strapping it to the body or to the head becomes almost a required action.

Remember, the idea is not to fight or attack from underwater. The idea is that Fukushima Ryu emphasizes the need to enter via unconventional routes. This means to enter through the mind of the enemy or to enter via poorly guarded routes. Water is, throughout human history, a poorly guarded route and thus ideal for shinobi insertion and exit. This device is meant to give shinobi-no-mono an advantage in water, thus making water insertion and extraction a more viable option.

I feel compelled to note that the device holds multiple breaths worth of air. Most of these breaths are taken in via the mouth, and expelled via the nostrils. However, the final breath can breathed into the pouch. That air can be rebreathed. It does have a higher content of carbon dioxide, but it also contains enough oxygen for one more breath. The idea that a rebreathed breath is toxic is as incorrect as it is absurd. Consider the principle of breathing in and out of a paper-bag to avoid hyperventilation. Consider that CPR breathing does not poison the unconscious person. You can inhale your exhaled breath without immediately passing out. It is the subsequent breaths after 1 or 2 rebreathed inhalations that will cause you to pass out.

Warning: Breathing beyond the one rebreathed breath will lead to blackout and drowning. There are tricks to breathing with this pouch that will allow a few extra rebreathed breaths, but I warn against the readers ever attempting them. These tricks must be trained in person and you run the risk of blacking out while studying them. While it is theoretically possible to breathe multiple rebreathed breaths, you should not risk it. As such, one should set themselves to a strict rule: "No more than 1 rebreathed breath."

One needs to be mindful of releasing all air from their lungs before they ascend. As you ascend, the pressure difference of air you inhaled underwater to the pressure of the air and water closer to the surface can cause severe damage to your lungs.

鹿ノ一足
"The small step of the Deer"

The root texts says:

"   *-Arsenic – 10 momme – collected from a silver mine*
-Young Japanese five-lined skink – 2 momme dried in the shade
-Botfly - 2 momme charred
-Root of Butterbur – 3 momme powdered and raw
- Cinnabar – five momme

This mixture is kept in thin paper."

The Annotations say: *"Powder the five colors. Put the mixture into a tissue paper, made of similar material to a tea bag. Carry this paper in folder handkerchief. If you disperse the contents to the enemy, the enemy will suffer hardship. They will become vulnerable to the ten directions. They may even die. Use caution to not to get any of the mixture on yourself. The drawing shows what the tissue paper should be like."*

This poison is named "鹿ノ一足". Similar to the "Knocking Down A Sword" spell, it is named after a martial arts technique, but it is NOT that technique. The name refers to taking someone down with an arm-bar, and then stepping on the back of their thigh before subduing them with a leg-lock and a hammer lock on their wrist. The idea here is that this poison is similar to the technique in that it will completely disorient the victim and leave them completely vulnerable. The name "鹿ノ一足" has many different meanings "The Deer's small step" or even "The Deer's stepping over another's legs". In some regard, the name can even signify "A Pairing of Two Deer". This technique is Jujutsu and can be found in many schools, with Tenshin Shoden Katori Shinto Ryu being one such school.

I will begin by saying that the key ingredients of this poison are the Arsenic and cinnabar. Simply put, the arsenic itself is sufficient to kill the individual. The cinnabar, which in this spell is Chinese cinnabar, adds to the lethality and makes the victim drowsy. Botflies are a parasitic fly, usually found infesting horses and horse feces. The butterbur can be poisonous is a few specific situations, but overall, it can add to drowsiness and fatigue of the target. The skink is a magical addition. Each of the five ingredients is associated with one of the five colors.

There, the Annotations need to be explained further. The Annotations mention dispersing the powder, but gives the sense of the powder being put into the air or even sprinkled onto the enemy. While this could easily work, it glosses over another method of dispersal, namely, placing the "tea-bag" into the inside of you're the enemy's clothing. Any form of wetness, such as rain, humidity, or even the enemy's own perspiration, will cause the arsenic (and other ingredients) to absorb into the skin.

Using "wet" in order to administer the poison also is in keeping with the fact that this poison was listed in-between the underwater breathing device and the boat (the "water" section of the manual).

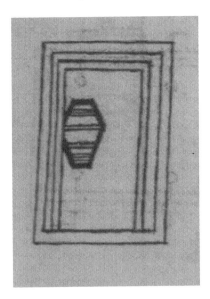

Again, while the other ingredients have their respective purposes, the main culprits in this technique are the arsenic and cinnabar.

堀渡舟之事
The Matter of the Moat Crossing Boat

The root text says "Boat for crossing a moat"

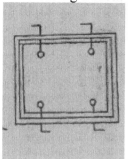

The Annotations say: *"The four pieces of the boat are in iruko style, with a cover like a traveling chest. The pieces of the boat can be taken out and connected to form a boat. These connections are made by latches which connect the boards. The oar is composed of pieces which connect in a manner similar to fishing poles."*

Iruko style means each box is successively smaller. Starting with the large box, each successive box can fit inside the previous box. These four pieces are fit inside each other and then covered with a top. This top is the same type of time found on a travelling box (hasamibako). This is a lid with metal u-shaped rings on top, which allow a long stick to be inserted. The box is then carried on the stick. The hasamibako is used for carrying clothes and would have been a common thing during the historic period. This would allow for the boat to be easily and covertly transported. When being carried, the entire boat becomes equal to a hasamibako.

The oar being "like a fishing rod" is similar to the iruko style of the boat. Traditional Japanese fishing rods were made from multiple pieces of bamboo of decreasing size. These different pieces would insert into each other to form a single pole (similar to modern day fishing poles). The oar is made the same way. The pieces of the oar could then be transported with the boat.

As the text says, the segments of the boat are connected via latches. These latches work better if they are not rounded, but rather, made of flat metal which locks into place.

The annotations seem to suggest that the pole and lid of the hasamibako are discarded during the usage of the boat. Here, I disagree with the Annotations and teach that an important aspect has been lost onTerasawa Sensei.

The pole that is used to carry the hasamibako can serve as part of the oar. The remaining portions of the oar are contained in the hasamibako. The lid of the hasamibako is also not discarded. The lid is used to cover one of the boxes, allowing one compartment of the boat to be protected from water. It can also serve as a seat. This is where one would carry items they would want to protect from getting wet during travel.

Pair this with the Arrow Stopper in times of great need.

浮沓之事
Floatation Device

The root text says: *"This is constructed a manner similar to the way a lantern with rings is made. It should be constructed with whale fin as the construction material. There is oral tradition for this device (kuden)."*

The Annotations say: *"Construct this device with leather treated with tung oil. It should be attached around koshigatana."*

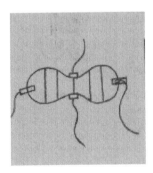

This same device appears in in the Kusunoki Ryu records numerous times, and is actually a fairly common device among the various shinobi traditions found throughout Japan. The *Shinobi Hiden* and *Bansenshukai* contain similar floatation devices. Kusunoki Masatora included a segment on these floatation devices in his guerilla war tactics manual. Within Masatora's work, these floatation devices are specifically mentioned in relationship to shinobi-no-mono operations in aquatic of swamp/marsh settings.

In Fukushima Ryu, the floatation device is crafted similar to a paper lamp. That is, a skeleton make of flexible rings, with a skin of whale and/or dolphin. Of course, other materials can be substituted. Even the basic construction can be altered if need be. However, the Fukushima Ryu tradition positions that the ring frame and whale/dolphin material works best.

Also, this version of the device has a secondary piece. This secondary piece is a second smaller floatation device (used for tools, sword, etc) which is attached to the main floatation device. In a bit of humor, my family often jokes that the floatation device comes with a cup holder. Jokes aside, the additional piece allows the koshigatana to be accessible. The normal version of the floatation device goes around the waist and obstructs easy access to the koshigatana. By having the koshigatana segmented to the side, it is easily accessible. When the Annotations say *"around the koshigatana"*, it means the main device around the waist and the secondary around the sword.

I also want to point out that the original text of the Annotations says "wakigatana". A wakigatana is a koshigatana. This can refer to a small katana, a tsuba-less small katana, and possibly even a wakizashi.

However, I will take this opportunity to introduce the reader to the fact that the House of Fukushima utilized a specialized type of weapon. This was a special type of koshigatana which was based on the Kusunoki Ryu. This koshigatana was called the "Kusunoki no Koshigatana". This type of weapon is a short blade with a small curved extension (a hook) near the handle. This style of blade has been erroneously associated with breaking helmets, but the reality is that the hook was used more for defense and disarming (defensive measures) than any offensive measures. Considering that it is very likely that this floatation device came from Kusunoki Ryu, it seems possible that the mentioned wakigatana, being a type of koshigatana, may be referring to this special type of weapon found among retainers of the House of Fukushima. Of course, it may not be referring to this weapon at all. Regardless of the exact weapon mentioned, the point is that one's personal weapon is given its own segment of flotation device, allowing the weapon to remain easily accessible.

Scroll Four

忍之火持之事
Covertly Holding Fire

The root text says:

"

-     *Charred culm sheaths of young bamboo – 1 momme 5 bu*
-     *Camphor – 4 bu*

Mix and solidify the mixture with thin glue. Cut the bamboo into a 5 sun section and make a hole in the end. When the mixture if perfect dry, push the mixture into the cylinder. Ignite the mixture on the open end. Doing it in this way will cause the fire to last fully for three days."

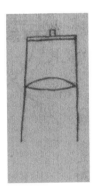

The Annotations say: *"Scrape the surface of the bamboo and apply tannin glue. The bamboo cylinder should have nodes on the top and the bottom. Pierce a hole in the joint on the bottom and forcefully push the mixture of the two ingredients tightly into the tube. Put a small hole on the top joint. This is also called '懐中火.'"*

"懐中火" means "Fire within your pocket". "懐" means "chest" and can refer to either the inner garment (underneath a kimono, for example) or directly to the inner pockets of any garment. The material compressed inside the tube will burn for three days. Furthermore, this burning can produce light, making this device a light source as well.

Furthermore, the tannin glue applied to the outside of the bamboo will provide a waterproof and thermal layer, protecting the flame inside and the user.

忍之薬
The Shinobi Medicine (Sleeping Powder)

The root text says:
"

- *Crow snake*
- *Hoya*
- *White snake*

Mix equal amounts of the ingredients and soak in oil for seven days. Air-dry the mixture. Powder the mixture and place it into a paper bag. Light the bag from a upwind direction."

The Annotations say:

"This is sleeping powder. 'Hoya' can be found on the roots of the (Asian) Wormwood. Put this powder in a paper bag with woven bamboo cover. Cover it with paper and tie it up with thread.

- *'crow snake' means black snake.*
- *'white snakes' means white snake*

If this burning substance travels downwind and over the enemy, everyone will fall asleep and this will create a gap, making it easier to steal in. You can prevent falling asleep from exposure to this method by putt the ginger (mentioned in part three) into your belly button. Use the device in the drawing."

In this medicine, "crow snake" is a black rat snake and the "white snake" is the Iwakuni white rat snake. The black and white snakes are highly significant in their relationship to In and Yo. Also, the powdered snake will "dampen wind". That is, these powdered snakes will slow the flow of Chi and cause the target to fall asleep. The Hoya, which is a type of root, further serves to knock out the target. In short, this medicine is a sleeping powder.

The Annotations go into the remedy of this powder, which was mentioned earlier. Ginger, freshly cut, gives your Chi enough of a boost ("flare up") that the effects of the powdered snake can be neutralized.

The diagram is a handheld tool used for preparing the ginger to counter the effects of the powder. One set of prongs is for holding while cutting, the other to hold while grating. The ginger is to be placed in your belly button and/or under your tongue.

In my own family, we still use this technique to address colds, flus, and a variety of other ailments. For example, if you have a bad cold or flu, put some ground up ginger in your belly button (and seal your belly button with a large band-aid) and place some sliced ginger under your tongue. This will also help to fight of fatigue and drowsiness.

手負ノ血留
Halting a Wound's Bleeding

The root text says:

"Fold paper to have eight layers.
Apply the folded paper, with pressure, to the wound.
There are oral traditions (kuden) for this, such as holding one's breath while performing this method."

The Annotations say: *"To cease the bleeding of wounded person, trace "款冬" (Japanese Yellow Rose) on the forehead of the injured person while holding your breath. After that, press the bleeding wound with paper and add pressure."*

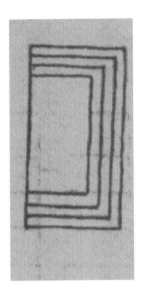

In this case, fold the paper eight times, like in the diagram. Then, hold your breath. This has an effect on your chi, but the full meaning is considered not something to put down in writing, even to this day.

The writing of "款冬" is symbolic of the meaning and spiritual functions relating to the Japanese Yellow Rose. Primarily, it is seen as a symbol of the transient nature of this world. There is a story where Ota Dokan was given a yellow rose by a young girl who could not afford to give him the raincoat she wished to provide for him. Initially, Ota Dokan was insulted by the gift, but later learned that it was given fully from her heart. This moved him to study poetry and contemplate the transient nature of the world. Later, when Ota Dokan was dying, his death poem was recorded as being *"Had I not known that I was already dead, I might have mourned my death."*

忍火手内二持事
The Matter of Covert Fire Held in the Palm of the Hand

The root text says:

"Use 8-9 quills of the feathers from a Japanese Crested Ibis. Cut the quills to the length of the width of your fist. Tie the quills together with string, forming a bundle. Pour mercury to quills, filling each quill about 8/10 of the way full."

The Annotations say:

"This is also called "round bright light" or "Covert Box". The box is 2 sun 9 bu and square. Its height is 2 sun 5 bu. Spread gold paint in a thin layer on the bottom of the box. Use up to five layers of gold leaf. Cut the spines of the feathers of a crested ibis to fit into the box. Make as many was will fill the box. Add mercury into the spines to a measurement of 8/10. Tie them together with thread and place this bundle in the box. You can use it for light whenever you want to observe something."

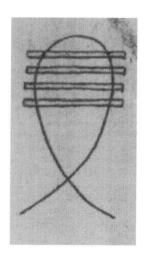

This is a topic which I have openly discussed on numerous occasions. Simply put, the mercury filled quills will glow a faint blue color due to the the minor electrical charge generated from the mercury moving among the internal structure of the quills. This is the same process that generates barometric light in barometers. Shaking the quils back and forth with cause the light to appear. With many quills, and a gold leaf covered box, enough light is generated to allow one to examine objects in the dark.

This is also known as "Yoshitsune Fire" and the "Undying Torch". This torch, as well as the "covert box", appears in the *Bansenshukai* as well.

忍返

Spikes on Top of Barriers

The root text only provides the following image:

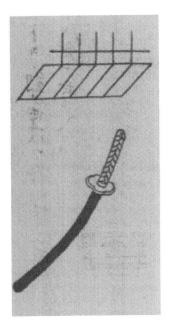

The Annotations state:

"This is about the spike on top of an outer wall. Throw the cord of your sword over the spikes. Hold onto the cord and cross over. Remember to use the hilt of your sword as a foothold."

This is the same as in the *Bansenshukai* and *Shoninki*.

壁外之火取事
Ember Carrier Outside the Walls

The root text says: *"Apply castor oil to twelve pieces of Yoshino paper and fold them.*
Dry in the shade for thirty days. You can see the light coming from the hole, which you can adjust to make it wider or narrower (as needed)."

The Annotations say: *"The diagram shows how to fold the paper."*

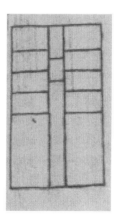

This is a paper ember carrier, created of origami-like interlocking pieces of folded paper. The ember carrier can be shrunk or extended to allow for various purposes.

Yoshino paper is special type of paper. The castor oil, when dried, will make the paper fire proof.

福嶋流心意工夫之巻
Fukushima Ryu - The Scroll of "Refining the Intention"

This closing scroll embodies the intentionality that Nojiri Narimasa considers the correct intentionality for a shinobo-no-mono. It encapsulates, in short direct fashion, the entire worldview of the shinobi. Within this small text is a considerable amount of commentary, of which I will only scratch the surface. Furthermore, a literal translation, considering the writing style of the author, is a poor choice for presenting the material to an English speaking audience. Many subtle aspects are simply lost. As such, I have taken slight liberty with the translation from the original Japanese in order to properly translate the actual meaning.

The root text begins:

"Shinobi-mono do not use magic in the beginning. Prior to any magic, shinobi-no-mono should first utilize the five constant factors and use wisdom, compassion, and brave tactics. If shinobi-no-mono attempt to obtain results with only magic, then they will be ensnared by delusions and lose Honshin. Shinobi-no-jutsu is an honorable thing.

This is a critical verse and serves four main functions.

1.) Magic is reserved for shinobi who have mastered the shinobi path, not for neophytes. That is, shinobi who are new to these arts must learn, study, and undergo a considerable amount of material and experience before they should ever consider using magic.

2.) There is a considerable amount of shinobi techniques not included in this manual. Since this manual focuses on magic and specialized tools, the manual does not address the "mundane and regular" shinobi skills. Namely, the manual does not address the espionage tactics.

3.) There are several principles which need to be integrated prior to magic usage. The five constant factors, wisdom, compassion, and brave tactics must all be integrated and permeate the mind of the shinobi before magic enters the equation. The term "brave tactics" also appears in Kusunoki Ryu when referring to espionage (see Kusunoki Ryu addendum).

4.) Honshin is both a goal and a measure of skill. Honshin means "correct mind". As a Buddhist term, it refers to the "primordial natural mind". This primordial natural mind is the same mind of Buddhahood. This mind is clear, calm, and free of conceptual and emotional stains. There is also a secondary meaning for Honshin. Honshin can also mean "the mind rooted in the topic". Thus, to have honshin means to not only have a "zen mind", but a mind that is rooted in the topic. Fukushima Ryu can, in theory, judge the quality of its students by the level of Honshin the student possesses.

The five constant factors are pulled directly from Sun Tzu's Tactics. They are:

1.) The Tao – This can be compared to morality among the society. This encompasses the "culture/sociology" of any given group. This covers all the social rules and the sense of harmony among the people. It should be understood that, when the people are in harmony and society functions well, the people are willing to follow a leader to the death. This is "culture" and "society".

2.) Heaven – This encompasses weather and the movement of heavenly bodies (sun, moon, and stars). This also covers night and day. This factor also encompasses dualism and movement. That is, this factor embodies "timing".

3.) Earth - This factor covers the various types of terrains (narrow terrain, deadly terrain, etc.). It also covers distance and geological factors. Simply put, all conflict takes place on the surface of this planet. The surface manifests as mountains, valleys, rivers, lakes, prairies, etc. The terrain covers the "setting" of any conflict, and this setting's impact on the conflict.

4.) General – The quality of the leader. This is found in the leader's level of wisdom, compassion, honesty, courage, and strictness. Personality of the leader also plays into this equation. This encompasses the entirety of force of the army being directed through the decisions of the generals. In short, this covers "direction".

5.) Law – This factor encompasses the ability of the army to maintain its ranks, maintain its moral, keep itself supplied, keep its infrastructure maintained, and properly hand out rewards and punishments. This is "logistics and organization".

These five factors apply to an armies and small groups, but can also be applied to an individual's mind. For an individual, it would manifest something like this:

1.) Tao: The culture and social conditioning of the individual

2.) Heaven: The timing of the individual, from chi flow and body functions, to the rise and fall of thoughts and emotions.

3.) Earth: The individual's body (bones, muscles, blood, etc) as well as their internal landscape. Memories, childhood trauma, hopes, fears, etc. will form a psychological landscape within the mind of the individual. This landscape can be traversed by skilled shinobi.

4.) General – The quality, or lack of quality, of the individual's morals and skills.

5.) Law – The individual's ability to manage himself. This comes in the form of possible spiritual vows, and the keeping or breaking of those vows. It also encompasses the individual's ability to govern themselves, such as managing their bank account and daily schedule.

Wisdom, Compassion, and Brave Tactics is a mixture of Sun Tzu's teachings, the *Six Secret Teachings*, and ideology present within the Kusunoki Ryu and Southern Court Loyalists.

1.) Wisdom – This does not mean simply memorizing and knowing many techniques and factoids. Rather, wisdom refers more to the ability to adapt and create solutions. Wisdom encompasses the Rational/Logical aspect.

2.) Compassion – This means empathy and the ability to always remember that human lives come first. When engaging in conflict, it is easy to forget the cost of human suffering. Compassion always keeps one properly aligned to the reality of human suffering. Compassion encompasses the Emotional/Humanity aspect.

3.) Brave Tactics – This term, within the context of Southern Court Loyalists (i.e. Kusunoki Ryu, the Nojiri of Fukushima Ryu, etc.), refers to espionage. Onchi Sakon uses the term "brave tactics" to refer to espionage and guerilla tactics in his manual, even using the term "man of brave tactics" to refer to spies in some instances.

Honshin, furthermore, should not be confused with simply having a calm mind. There is a distinct difference between a mundane calm mind and Honshin. Honshin is related to the primordial nature, where-as a mundane calm mind is still completely bound by ignorance. Honshin does have the "side-effect" of making one calm and relaxed, in the sense that one is not fettered by constant conceptual and emotional entanglements. However, Honshin also allows the wisdom of the primordial nature to flow into the present experience. Mundane calm mind does not.

The root text continues:

"Shinobi-no-mono observe the enemy with the element of surprise, and by working independently, in the dark of night, they strike at the insubstantial. One follows intuition, with faith, and reaches the truth."

"Observe the enemy" refers to the shinobi scouting out the enemy. The shinobi watch not only from the outside, like a traditional scout,

but they observe from within the enemy ranks (as a spy). The shinobi is always watching and analyzing the enemy. Observation is a fundamental skill of the shinobi-no-mono.

"... element of surprise..." refers to the fact that the shinobi must always remain hidden. The enemy must never know they are victims of a shinobi plot.

"... working independently..." refers to the fact that shinobi operate independent from the army. While there are many other types of warriors in old Japanese armies which were similar to shinobi, such as scouts and ambushers, only the shinobi operated with complete independence. The Shinobi-no-samurai (Ninshi) would receive an assignment and then disappear into the enemy territory. Communication went from the Ninshi back to high ranking generals, if not the Lord himself. This allowed the shinobi an incredible amount of freedom. However, it also means the shinobi must have an incredible sense of internal discipline and an extremely developed skill set. Since most Ninshi recruit citizens of the enemy's territory to do their bidding, the Ninshi must also learn to not become attached to the people they recruit. At the end of the operation, most of those people will be dead, abandoned, or, at a minimum, separated from the Ninshi. The Ninshi must learn to remain "independent", even when working with dozens of other people. The shinobi-no-mono, in that regard, must learn to be alone.

"...in the dark of night..." refers not only to nighttime operations, but to the overall aspect that the ninja operates where they cannot be seen. Shinobi operate in the gap of the enemy's attention, that is, where the enemy is not paying attention and is not capable of perceiving the movement. The dark of night is a poetic representation of this principle.

"...strike at the insubstantial..." The usage of insubstantial is for the sake of translation. The actual kanji is *"void"* but also can mean *"crack"* or "gap" (this was mentioned previously).This is extremely important, because there is a double meaning. The first meaning, "insubstantial/empty", refers to the aspects of the enemy which are not physical. Namely, it refers to attacking the enemy's mind and heart. The shinobi attacks the emotionality of the enemy. The

shinobi attacks the mind and thoughts of the enemy. The shinobi causes faithful retainers to abandon their master. The shinobi causes the enemy commander to become paranoid and jump at ghost, making horrible decisions and leaving the enemy army powerless. The second meaning, *"crack"*, refers to shinobi ideology. Namely, that shinobi slip into the enemy via the small cracks and holes/spaces in the enemy's defenses. The word *"strike"* is key because we must always remember that the shinobi doesn't simply slip into the enemy's mind for random reasons. The shinobi slips into the enemy's mind with the specific purpose of attacking the enemy from the inside.

"One follows intuition, with faith, and reaches the truth." refers to a complex concept, which I will attempt to explain succinctly. Intuition, here, does not refer to mundane intuition. It refers to intuition born from Honshin. That is, it is the gut instincts born from a combination of calm mind and wisdom. This form of intuition is expressed and channeled through years of experience, in particular, experience born from espionage work. Once this intuition begins to blossom in the mind of the shinobi, the shinobi should follow it. The term *"... with faith..."* means that the shinobi must be have faith in this intuition. Furthermore, it means that the shinobi must be faithful to their side during the conflict. Intuition becomes the vessel and faith becomes the pathway. When the shinobi rides upon their intuition down the tunnel of faith, then they will arrive at truth. This faith can also mean faith in the enlightened mind.

This is a very profound point, because the shinobi's world is filled with deception. Ironically, it is for this exact reason (a world of deception) that the shinobi must hold unwaveringly to their intuition and faith. The shinobi starts at a place of light and travels through darkness to arrive at light (the truth) again. This principle is known as "leading the light". Ideologically, the shinobi's heart is a light which is lead through the darkness to arrive at the light of truth on the other side of the darkness.

This is why Nojiri concludes this portion with the statement that *"Shinobi-no-jutsu is an honorable thing."* Shinobi arts may look dark and evil from the outside, but when a shinobi's intention is refined, shinobi arts are actually nothing but the light of wisdom and compassion. In Buddhism, it is known as "skillful means".

Skillful Means (Sanskrit: Upaya) is the clever methods of compassion and wise beings in order to pacify suffering in this world. The classic example is of a father lying to his children to get them to leave a dangerous situation. In this example, the house is on fire, but the children do not comprehend the danger and will not leave. The father then tells the children that he has many toys and goodies outside. The children then rush outside to chase after the goodies, and they are saved from the flames. Such lies are not considered negative actions, but rather, they are considered a form of clever wisdom. This is the type of mentality that Nojiri is instructing the shinobi to have: Clever wisdom. This is how to refine one's intentionality so that their heart stays pure. This is precisely why black magic is forbidden to neophytes, as the shinobi path must be refined before the temptations and beguiling influence of black magic can even be attempted.

The root text continues:

"Correct bravery should not be restrained while brute courage should be admonished. Caution should be applied, as it is a medicine for easing one's situation."

The Kusunoki Ryu texts discuss this dualism many times. Correct bravery refers to a committed and focused mind that is dedicated to the cause despite all personal harm. The strength of this bravery comes from patience, acceptance, and commitment. Brute Courage is reckless bravery. That is, it is limited and subject to quick burnout. It is egotistical and unreliable, because it lacks acceptance and commitment. Brute courage spoils plots and gets agents killed.

The caution being applied is a crucial piece of instruction. Many samurai were taught to throw caution to the wind and rush headfirst into a glorious death. Nojiri is teaching the exact opposite. Nojiri is saying that one should utilize a level of caution (a level of caution which might be construed as cowardly by non-shinobi) when engaging in covert operations. The application of this caution becomes like a medication to calm your mind. That is, one can relax and be at ease because they are allowed to slow down, be cautious, and be mindful. In short, the shinobi is not expected to be an enemy-rushing hero. The shinobi is expected to be a shadow, pulling strings from behind the scenes. This relieves the shinobi of social expectations. Furthermore, when one becomes accustomed to being cautious, the habit of caution will keep them safe, this inducing a level of ease into their life (avoiding problems = easier life).

The root text continues:

"Mastering these skills, in addition to the set of principles, your chi will be enhanced and benefits will be acquired."

By mastering shinobi arts and the principles discussed, one's chi will be enhanced (strengthened) and benefits will be acquired. This single line has the potential to be developed into an entire book. However, the full scope of Chi and acquiring the benefits of increased Chi is beyond the scope of this book. We will briefly cover some of the dynamics.

First, one must understand that Chi is the movement of the mind. On a profound level, the mind, non-dual with Emptiness (discussed below), radiates the five colors/elements. These elements manifest as various forms in this world. Chi is the movement of these lights/elements. It is through these movements that changes take place.

On a medium level, Chi is the "energy" which allows for spiritual powers. Higher Chi allows one to see Chi clouds and ghosts, and allows one to empower their paper spells. Strong chi allows one to launch curses and counter-curses. Strong chi defends against ghosts, while weak chi succumbs to ghostly attacks.

On a basic level, Chi means "attention". When Chi is strong, our attention is sharper and faster. This also means that our body is functioning healthy. The Shinobi Medicine and the Ginger root, mentioned previously, interact with our Chi on this level. The snake skins subdue Chi flow and the ginger increases Chi flow. Thus, our attention is dampened or increased with such things.

The root text continues:

*"Defeating the enemy army is a matter of contemplation and using
the established path. Severing the enemy's plans is the highest
military art. However, in a needy situation, you may need to attack.
However, obtaining benefits in this way is not a skillful methodology.
Even the courage of a humble man, you can achieve 100 victories
out of 100 conflicts if you act in accordance with the principle of
Shunyata. Honshin will not be lost and one will secure benefits."*

The beginning lines are, essentially, a portion of Sun Tzu's Tactics
rearranged. When Nojiri says *"defeating an army"*, he is not
discussing the act of beating an enemy with physical force. He is
discussing the act of truly removing the enemy army's potential to
do harm to your forces. Within the "intentionality of shinobi", this
means that the enemy has become a victim of your spy network.
Valid and authentic information regarding the enemy flows freely,
and the enemy has mistakenly believed any and all disinformation
campaigns charged against them. When the enemy is permeated by
your spies, they have been defeated.

This is not the result of divine intervention, spirits, or luck. While
those magical things can be used to some extent, this victory is based
purely on successful espionage. Successful espionage depends upon
"contemplation", that is, intensive planning and analyzing of all
factors involved. Furthermore, it involves using the *'established
path'*. Again, this has a double meaning. The first meaning is that
one needs to use all of the established ideologies and techniques of
shinobi. One does not need to recreate "ninjutsu", one simply needs
to use it. This is similar to a painter not needing to recreate the
methods of painting. They simply need to just paint. The second
aspect is that *'established path'* refers to the paths laid down by the
enemy. One does not need to worry or struggle to make pathways
into the enemy's mind. Rather, one observes the enemy and the
pathways into their mind will naturally express themselves.

"Severing the enemy's plans is the highest military art" is taken directly from Sun Tzu's Tactics. In the original Japanese text, the kanji (伐謀) mirrors the line from Sun Tzu's Tactics. In the third chapter, Sun Tzu says that *"Severing the enemy's plans is the highest military art. Second is keeping the enemy from unifying. Third is attacking the enemy. Last is sieging walled cities."* Thus, we see further into the mindset of a shinobi-no-mono of this tradition. Severing the enemy's plans is positioned as the primary goal. However, this counterattacking, in this case, must be understood properly. Another way to translate this phrase is the say *"counterattacking the enemy's tactics before the enemy can launch the tactics"*.

Severing the enemy's plans, or countering the enemy's tactics, is the result of espionage. The shinobi would have undergone an extensive campaign to have done as much as possible to disable the enemy's capabilities. Ideally, the campaign would have reduced the enemy's ability to proceed with any hostilities. However, in the real world, the probability of succeeding to this extent is rare. Even after having reduced the enemy's capabilities, the enemy will probably still attack. This is when counterattacking tactics manifest. During the campaign to reduce the enemy's capabilities, a system of preparing counterattack mechanisms would also be put into effect. The enemy's plans, tactics, ambush points, supply points, and various other key factors, will all be known by the shinobi and their leaders. The enemy, with already weakened capabilities, will walk into their own defeat. When they attack, they seal their fate. This is like trapping the enemy in an iron box, leaving only a small hole to exit. When the enemy tries to slip through this very small hole, you are waiting outside of the box with an executioner's axe, ready to sever their head the moment they begin to exit the box.

In conjunction with the second meaning of *'established paths'*, counterattacking the plans can also manifest this second meaning, which is based on the pathways laid down by the enemy themselves. In other words, counterattacking the enemy's plans has a three-step process:

1.) The enemy's habits and behaviors lay down *"established paths"*.

2.) The shinobi operates within these 'established paths', using the enemy's own world as the raw material to build the campaign

3.) When the enemy finally attacks, their own movement is the very conductor of the counterattack. Like a special kind of knot around their throat, each time they move, the knot tightens more.

However, Nojiri understands that this is not always the situation. Many times, one has to move to attack. Various reasons can force one's hands into attacking first. Perhaps the covert campaign has been discovered or maybe the enemy has suddenly, and unpredictably, begun moving and time has suddenly shifted into the enemy's favor. Several reasons can force the shinobi to shift from spies to commandos, but when this happens, one can be assured that victory is still possible in this situation.

What comes next is a very profound lesson, and it begins with the expression *"Even with the courage of a humble man..."* This is to reiterate that a shinobi must have the proper courage and continues to admonish brute courage or reckless bravery. The courage of a humble man connects to the "caution" mentioned previously. One does not need any particular or special type of courage. One simply needs the courage of a humble man, that is, a common everyday man.

The line of winning *"100 victories out of 100 conflicts"* comes straight from Sun Tzu's Tactics. However, we must remember that Sun Tzu teaches that the 100 victories are not a display of skill. Of course, winning 100 times out of 100 times is desirable, but the true skill is found in the plan dismantling mentioned earlier. However, as the world is as it is, when the proper factors required for such victory are not possible to assemble, then conflict ensues. When this conflict ensues, even humble and common men can win 100 out of 100 battles.

Again, this is a double edge sword. It confirms that a shinobi can win whenever things go wrong. However, that having been said, it reminds the shinobi that, regardless of the ability to win, the overall quality/skill of the operation and those involved has decreased. This is an insight into the shinobi's ideology. The shinobi trains and becomes proficient in guerilla warfare and commando tactics for when operations go sour, but this measure also carries a level of failure.

At this point, Nojiri begins to veer away from the standard teaching found in the Sun Tzu's Tactics by adding the extremely important line *"... with the Principle of Shunyata."* Shunyata is the Sanskrit word for *"Emptiness"*, a Buddhist teaching.

Shunyata is, ultimately, inexpressible in words and a full analysis of Shunyata is beyond the scope of this book. In short, Shunyata means:

- Nothing has an inherent identity
- All phenomena are empty of any permanent identifying qualities
- All phenomena are without an inherit self
- All phenomena are constantly in changing
- Nothing can be held onto
- All thoughts and emotions are illusions/delusions
- All things exist in interdependence
- Everything is comprised of factors which temporarily come together and, eventually, break apart

The more profound Buddhist teachings go more in-depth on Shunyata, with the higher teachings explaining that all phenomena are the non-duality of the mind itself and Shunyata. Esoteric Buddhism explains that the five Buddha families are the natural radiance of the Shunyata. Shunyata is the fundamental reason for the existence of magic, and Nojiri's mentioning it further cements Shunyata as one of the fundamental principles of Fukushima Ryu. It should also be noted that Kusunoki Ryu's magical teachings are rooted in Shunyata (see the Kusunoki Ryu addendum).

In an applicable aspect, Shunyata and the integration of Shunyata into the shinobi's life is the underlying principle which allows the shinobi to have a creative mind. The shinobi frees their mind from countless layers of concepts and limitations. The shinobi allows countless thoughts and emotions to simply appear and disappear from their mind stream, viewing them as empty apparitions. With such training, the shinobi is not limited to options. The shinobi can shift identities, take on new forms, new accents, and new habits. In terms of tactics, the shinobi can escape the aforementioned "iron box" by simply refusing to play by the rules of the physics of the iron box. Instead of escaping through the small hole, the shinobi merely walks through the walls, because their mind is empty of the "rules".

Nojiri, by saying that the principle of Shunyata is the reason for winning 100 battles out of 100 battles, relieves the shinobi of the shame of failing to achieve a clean victory. That is, Nojiri is telling the student to actually not worry about Sun Tzu's admonishments, but to simply win the battle if it comes down to it. The text then goes on to say that Honshin will not be lost. It should be clear that Honshin will not be lost when the victory is achieved with Shunyata. This further develops both options:

1.) Achieve victory without Shunyata: Lower military skill, not very impressive. Honshin is not retained. Victory is sloppy and at great cost.

2.) Achieve victory with Shunyata: A higher path. Honshin is maintained. Victory is clean and at a reduced cost.

The root text concludes with:

"The proceeding scroll is the foundation of Shinobi and contains the essential elements needed in refining your mind. The previous four scrolls contain those elements that are magical, as well as including some logical skills.

Nojiri Jiroemon Narimasa
Okita Sukeshiro Naomichi
Nojiri Saburoemon Masatsugu
Okimi Jirobei
Miyake Juzo"

This summarizes the root text. The first four scrolls contained magic and specialized tools. The final scroll presents the foundation for Shinobi-no-jutsu and the view to refine one's intention.

The first signature belongs to Nojiri Narimasa, the author of the manual and leader of the Nojiri family members tasked with forming Fukushima Ryu. Nojiri Masatsugu took control of the system later on. This particular copy got as far as Miyake Juzo, who took control of the system after the House of Fukushima was established in Nagano. The final documented master of Fukushima Ryu (not contained in this list) was Murakami Sensei, in Nagano in the 1800s.

The House of Nojiri had our own ninjutsu prior to forming the Fukushima Ryu and after the House of Nojiri drifted away from the House of Fukushima. Fukushima Ryu had two major drifts. The official line continued in the House of Fukushima in Nagano. A few unofficial lines floated around Western Japan (where the Annotations seem to have been written).

After the House of Fukushima was reduced and moved from Hiroshima to Nagano, Kumazawa Morihisa stayed with Fukushima Masanori until Masanori's death. After Masanori's death, Kumazawa Morihisa went on to serve the Matsudaira (Tokugawa). The House of Nojiri began to stretch far, with many members becoming employed by the House of Nakagawa, some by the House of Kato and some by the House of Hachisuka. Many Nojiri relied on the House of Nojiri for support and worked as ronin. Nojiri Kazutoshi, who Kumazawa Morihasa gave his daughter in marriage, worked as a ronin and used the various land holdings of the House of Nojiri as bases of operations. Nojiri Kazutoshi's son, Kumazawa Banzan, would go on to become one of the three great Confucian scholars of the Edo period. The Nojiri who served the House of Hachisuka continued to engage in espionage. In the 1800s, my own family was serving as personal retainers to the karo (House Elders).

Thus, the Fukushima Ryu Shinobi-no-Maki shows insight into this type of ninjutsu, but is by no means a complete presentation. As such, I advise the readers to understand that there is a considerable amount of information simply not contained within the original scroll or this commentary.

The Annotations say:

"

仁 *Compassion*
義 *Morality*
礼 *Social Manners*
智 *Wisdom*
信 *Faith*

Conduct yourself with these virtues

Written on an auspicious day of the fourth month in the summer 1797 (Year of the Snake) by the 8th grandchild of Hyogo-ryo, Terasawa Naosaku Yukihiro.

Transmitted to Ishikawa Yamato Minamoto Asomi Mitsunori as a cherished treasure.
Transcribed on an auspicious morning of the tenth month in the winter of 1824 (Year of the Monkey). "

Here we have an error in the Annotations. The five constant factors are as explained above. However, the author of the Annotations has fallen victim to socio-political realities. In the later Edo period, Confucian thinking replaced much of the original teachings. Sun Tzu taught the five constant factors as Tao, Heaven, Earth, General, and Law. However, Confucius taught a different set, the set listed in the Annotations. There is a critical error here, because not only is this set NOT the set intended by Nojiri Narimasa, but the Confucian set is meant to apply to peacetime, not armies and wartime operations.

Thus, this is a genuine mistake, due to the author of the Annotations failing to consider the context of Nojiri's writing. It is unclear if this error is the author's error, or if that line of Fukushima Ryu was degrading. Considering the Annotations were written in 1797, it may be very possible that the mistake is due to the system having degraded over 200 years.

As matters of cultural importance, the words "Hyogo-ryo" and "Asomi" are court rank titles. When the text says *"8ᵗʰ grandchild of*

Hyogo-ryo", it means 8th lineal descendant. It is believed that "Hyogo-ryo" is referring to Terasawa Katataka, who was a daimyo of the Karatsu Domain in the late 1500s. His court title was Hyogo-ryo (兵庫頭) and his rank was the "Lower 5th". At the time, his koku intake was around 120,000 koku. The author of the Annotations is a descendent of this man. The House of Terasawa served as the daimyo of Karatsu until the mid-1600s.

It should also be noted that the Karatsu Domain was what is also called Hizen Province. This is the same territory that many Nojiri, such as Nojiri Kazutoshi, were working as ronin during the Edo period. Also, some of Nojiri Kazutoshi's grandchildren served the House of Nakagawa in the neighboring province of Bungo in the late 1600s.

So, what we see is the existence of the Fukushima Ryu being studied, used, and passed down outside of the House of Fukushima and, seemingly, far from Nagano. It is currently unknown how many transmissions took place outside of the main line.

We should also take note that these Annotations were transcribed in 1824, showing that, even in the 1800s, these manuals were still being transcribed and passed down.

CHAPTER 4

ADDENDUM:
A Brief Survey of Kusunoki Ryu

This brief survey is a concise overview of the phenomenon known as "Kusunoki Ryu". As such, not every detail is revealed out within these pages, nor is the presented material fully explored. I have attempted to provide a solid overview of the history, philosophy, and mechanics of the system, as well as the people involved in its creation and maintenance. However, I would be lying if I told you that this survey is the final word on the topic. Hopefully, future researchers will build on this material and reveal even more information and insights.

This having been said, I would then say that this survey is one of the first times that this much information regarding Kusunoki Ryu has been revealed in English. The total amount of information related to Kusunoki Ryu is immense. Thus, more than just listing hundreds of techniques, I have chosen to provide the reader with an insight into the context of Kusunoki Ryu. The primary context of Kusunoki Ryu is, and always was, the idea of a revitalization of the Southern Court. Even though several branches of Kusunoki Ryu formed over hundreds of years, they all stem from the original intention of revitalizing Go-Daigo's line. It was not until the ideal of a revitalization of the Southern Court began to seriously fade that the system of Kusunoki Ryu began to fade. As the collection of systems lost the original intention, the collective known as "Kusunoki Ryu" eventually faded into the pages of history.

Perhaps by showing some of the system, within its original intentionality, some life might find its way back into the system, if only as a vivid and cherished piece of Japanese history.

Understanding the Basics

As with most topics of study, it is best to begin with the fundamental details. In this case, this means understanding the origin of the system.

Kusunoki Ryu is actually a collection of numerous related systems. While each of the systems all stem from Kusunoki Masashige, each system branches off into its own respective lineages. Some of these branches became involved with other systems (such as Fukushima Ryu), while some of them stayed independent. Some of these systems served a political function, some did not.

The Founder

The founder of all authentic Kusunoki Ryu systems was Kusunoki Masashige. Kusunoki Masashige has been misrepresented by historians and authors throughout the years. Sometimes on purpose, but mostly out of ignorance. Many historians say that he was the leader of a group of roving bandits and that his skill was used by Emperor Go-Daigo because the Emperor needed a wily warrior to do his dirty work. This is extremely far from the truth.

Kusunoki Masashige was born among warriors who owned the Kawachi province (Eastern portion of Osaka). He studied Buddhism, reading, writing, and various other disciplines at a local Shingon temple until the age of 14. At 14, he began studying Heiho (Military Strategy). The Heiho he studied is known as the "Seven Chinese Classics". The three main texts he studied out of the seven were the *Sun Tzu Heiho, the Six Secret Teachings, and the Three Strategies.* In fact, an analysis of the Kusunoki Ryu root texts show the correlation between Kusunoki Ryu tactics and the tactics found in these manuals. Specifically, as will be shown further in this survey, there is a very strong connection between the teachings of Kusunoki Ryu and the *Six Secret Teachings*.

During the early 1300s, Emperor Go-Daigo launched a campaign to wrestle the country back from the grips of the Hojo Clan's Military-Industrial stranglehold. Prior to Go-Daigo, the Hojo Clan had succeeded in ripping power from the Minamoto Shogun. From that point, the Hojo Clan systematically abused their power and authority to establish a police state. Emperor Go-Daigo, refusing to let the country be used as a puppet for Hojo interests, launched his Kemmu Restoration. For this, the service of Kusunoki Masashige was secured.

It is important to understand the details of the Kemmu Restoration and the various battles Kusunoki Masashige won and lost, because it was through these conflicts that the Kusunoki Ryu was born. Kusunoki Masashige did not inherit the system. He created it from the experience of these battles. As one studies the Kusunoki Ryu root texts, they see reference to these battles. In some cases, Kusunoki Masashige developed a strategy in direct response to a threat, and it worked so well, that the technique became part of the system.

Kusunoki Masashige died soon after the Kemmu Restoration, when a general named Ashikaga Takauji betrayed Emperor Go-Daigo. This betrayal began the Nanbokucho War, in which the legitimate court of Emperor Go-Daigo was forced to combat a false puppet court created by the Ashikaga Clan. The legit court was named the Southern Court (Nancho) and the fraudulent court was known as the Northern Court. The Northern Court resided in Kyoto and the Southern Court in Yoshino.

As explained previously, this war between the North and South continued for centuries. While most historians erroneously state that it ended in the 1390s, the truth (supported by solid historical evidence) is that the war continued indefinitely. Disputes between the North and South continued even into the 1980s. Occasionally, even to this present day, some minor flare ups regarding the issue briefly reveal themselves. It is important to know that the issue of the Northern and Southern courts is a key concern to the main Kusunoki Ryu. Restoration of the authentic Emperor is a foundational aspect of the entire system. Many of the branch lineages, before they diluted from this original intention, were heavily focused on this objective.

Before he died, Kusunoki Masashige entrusted the system to his sons, Masatsura and Masanori, as well as their bodyguard and chief spy, Onchi Sakon. As history would have it, Masatsura would die young, but Masanori and the Onchi family survived the Nanbokucho wars. With them, the main Kusunoki Ryu line and branches (such as Koyo Ryu and Onchi Ryu) survived as well.

As time progressed, the teachings and original intentionality would branch off into various systems and families. In some cases, the original teachings and original intentionality stayed intact, while in many cases it became diluted.

The Main Lineages

The main branches of the system are: Kusunoki Masanori Ryu, Kusunoki Shigeyuki Ryu, Taiheiki Ryu, Kawachi Ryu, Koyo Ryu, Onchi Ryu, and Shin-Kusunoki Ryu.

It is the opinion of the author that Fukushima Ryu should be listed as a descendant of Kusunoki Ryu.

The following is a brief break-down of these systems:

- **Kusunoki Masanori Ryu**: This is the primary Kusunoki Ryu. For most purposes, the generalized name of "Kusunoki Ryu" or "Kusunoki Ryu Gungaku" refers to Kusunoki Masanori Ryu. The ultimate fate of this line is disputed.
- **Kusunoki Shigeyuki Ryu**: This is a branch of the main line.
- **Taiheiki Ryu**: A branch of the main line propagated by the Imagawa family. Two volumes of the Kusunoki Ryu Kaden root text were written by the Imagawa.
- **Kawachi Ryu**: A branch that produced several key manuals and texts.
- **Onchi Ryu**: An early branch of Kusunoki Masanori Ryu. The Onchi family inherited a variation of Kusunoki Masanori Ryu. While the main line stayed with the Kusunoki family, the Onchi family began their own cadet branch.
- **Koyo Ryu**: When the Onchi taught their variation of Kusunoki Ryu to the Akamatsu family, the Akamatsu family produced their own line. There is some debate as to if their branch is just Onchi Ryu with a new name, or if Koyo Ryu contains its own distinct material.
- **Shin-Kusunoki Ryu**: This is also known as Natori Ryu. The Natori family served the Kishu Tokugawa. During the later 1600s, a Natori strategist studied Kusunoki Ryu Gungaku that descended from Kusunoki Fuden. The Kishu lord asked

Natori to mix Kusunoki Fuden's material with Natori Ryu and rename the system Shin-Kusunoki Ryu. However, the name change did not stick and the system was reabsorbed under the banner of Natori Ryu.

- **Fukushima Ryu**: Many historians would not agree that I have added Fukushima Ryu to this list, but my reason is rooted in rational thinking and logic. We know that the Fukushima Ryu was formed by the House of Nojiri/Kumazawa. We know that the Kumazawa line was the actual Southern Imperial line and that the Nojiri were personal retainers and relatives to the Imperial Line. We know that the Nojiri were directly related to the House of Yasumi (via adoptions and marriages). The House of Yasumi served under Kusunoki Masashige and Kusunoki Masanori directly. We also know that the Yasumi and Nojiri alliance controlled Iimori castle after the Onchi family faded from history. Furthermore, the Nojiri/Yasumi moved in the same circles that Kusunoki Masatora (inheritor of the main line) moved within. An interaction between the two is both possible and probable. With Fukushima Ryu being founded by such a heritage, I believe it is a fair assessment to consider the system part of the Kusunoki Ryu collective.

I would like to point out at this time that there are other schools that claim to either be Kusunoki Ryu or have a connection to Kusunoki Ryu. Some of these connections are valid, but some of them are either highly questionable or have no verifiable validity at all.

For example, many researchers claim that the House of Takeda inherited Kusunoki Ryu. While there is an aspect of truth to this statement, outside of context, this truth can be misleading. The Takeda did NOT have the main branch of Kusunoki Ryu (i.e. Kusunoki Masanori Ryu). However, the House of Takeda absolutely did have portions of Onchi Ryu and Koyo Ryu integrated into their warfare systems.

The main Kusunoki Ryu line stayed with a man named Kusunoki Masatora, who was a retainer for Oda Nobunaga. It was within the ranks of Oda Nobunaga's army that the original and main branch was spread. One cannot but help speculate if this factor played a large role in Oda's intelligence networks and warfare strategies. Perhaps Oda Nobunaga was so successful due to the presence of Kusunoki Ryu practitioners within his army?

Concerning Natori Ryu, it is generally accepted that Kusunoki Fuden taught Kusunoki Ryu Gungaku. Natori Ryu absorbed teachings from Kusunoki Ryu Gungaku. However, the exact lineage of Kusunoki Fuden remains a mystery. Many historians believe that Kusunoki Fuden inherited his teachings from Kusunoki Masatora. Unfortunately, this is only an assumption. No real evidence has surfaced to support the assumption. In fact, if we wanted to be very critical, we could say that even the identity of Kusunoki Fuden is debatable.

However, we can see Kusunoki Ryu's footprints all over Natori Ryu. The material taught by Yui Shosetsu (Kusunoki Fuden's successor) is clearly influenced by Kusunoki Ryu. Although, I must admit, it looks influenced—not a direct inheritance--- by the Kusunoki Masanori Ryu (the main line). As such, it is the opinion of the author that Fuden's material does not come from the main line. This assumption comes from a survey of Yui Shosetsu's own works, not Natori Ryu manuals. Concerning Natori Ryu manuals, we would naturally expect to see Kusunoki Ryu existing only as footprints within the system, considering that we know the root system is a system other than Kusunoki Ryu.

Other historians have produced work in recent years which have clearly shown that Natori Ryu was developed by the Natori family while the Natori served under the House of Takeda and maintained a good relationship with the Sanada Family. These findings further conclude that Natori Ryu should not be considered a root Kusunoki Ryu tradition, but rather, its own tradition with an influence from Kusunoki Fuden's lineage. That is, a descendant of Kusunoki Ryu. As such, its texts cannot be considered root texts. Similarly, the author believes that Yui Shosetsu's works must be considered outside the root text collection as well.

Fukushima Ryu should equally be considered a descendant tradition, not a root tradition, of Kusunoki Ryu. It is also the opinion of the author that the House of Takeda, which is often hailed as being inheritors of Kusunoki Ryu, should be relegated to "descendant branch" and not be given the title of "root branch".

Out of all the traditions, the only systems which should be considered to have produced root texts are those systems which directly contributed to the root texts of the Taiheiki Hidensho (to be discussed in the following section). This means that we will be considering the texts, primarily, of Kusunoki Masanori Ryu, Onchi Ryu, Kawachi Ryu and Taiheiki Ryu.

The Source Material (Manuals)

For this survey, I have chosen to utilize the following manuals. Most of these densho come from the main source material, that is, the root text collection of the main Kusunoki Ryu line. I have also included some manuals which are descendants of the roots text collection, as their existence and teaching are substantive and worth including for a more developed understanding.

Taiheiki no Hidensho
(Also known as *Taiheiki Hiden* and a few other names)

Opposed the standard Taiheiki, written by Northern Court historians, the Southern Court Loyalist have their own Taiheiki. This alternate Taiheiki is not a single document, but rather, a collection of numerous documents. This set has various names, with a few variations in the collection contents. This arrangement of texts is known as the Taiheiki Hidensho. While there is some debate among various traditions as to the contents of this collection, we will work with the most well known version, known as Taiheiki Hiden Rijin Sho.

It is this collection that forms the root texts and the supplementary text of the various Kusunoki Ryu lineages. As stated, each lineage has some variation of the documents contained within the collection. In generalized theory, the collection begins with works from Kusunoki Masashige and Onchi Sakon. Over the centuries, various authors have added material. To be clear to the reader, the texts surveyed in this book come from the Taiheiki Hiden.

It is important to note that this root text collection is not called "Kusunoki Ryu Manuals", but rather, even the name and presentation continues to express loyalty and devotion to the Southern Court. This has cultural and political implications, as many Kusunoki Ryu practitioners were either Southern Court guerrillas, supported the guerillas, or were at least part of some sort of significant uprising related to the politics of the Southern Court loyalists.

Onchi no Maki
(Also known as *Taiheiki Onchi no Maki* and a few other names)

Written by Onchi Sakon, this manual is a collection of various sayings and strategies of Kusunoki Masashige, along with recorded memories and theories of Onchi Sakon himself. It was written later in the Nanbokucho Wars. An exact date is unknown. Based on the content of the manual, it appears to have been written, at the earliest, in the late 1340s.

Onchi Sakon was Kusunoki Masashige's chief spy. Some historians record his death in 1336, but this appears to be erroneous. Several Southern Court records show him alive and well after 1336. According to the Onchi no Maki, he was tasked with caretaking Kusunoki Masatsura and Masanori. He was also tasked with helping these two learn their father's techniques. Onchi Sakon also continued to serve as a chief espionage officer. Within the Kusunoki root texts, we see writings of Onchi Sakon well beyond 1336, with his death occurring around the late 1360s.

It should be mentioned here that Onchi Sakon is mentioned several times in the famous ninja manual *Bansenshukai*.

Kusunoki Kaden

This text is a collection of seven volumes of works from Imagawa Nyodo, Kusunoki Masashige, Kusunoki Masatora and Onchi Sakon. The first two volumes were written by Imagawa Nyodo, followed by material written by Kusunoki Masatora (head of the main line in the 1500s), a few volumes written by Kusunoki Masashige (under a court title name), and the final volume written by Onchi Sakon.

Imagawa Shinsei Nyodo lived in the later 1400s. He wrote several documents in conjunction with Kusunoki Ryu and the Southern Court guerilla forces. He added several volumes of writings to the Taiheiki Hidensho collection. It was also Imagawa Shinsei Nyodo who appeared to begin heavy use of the words "shinobi no mono" and "shinobi no tsuwamono", whereas the older manuals use other words to refer to espionage operatives.

The following two pages show some examples of Imagawa's writings.

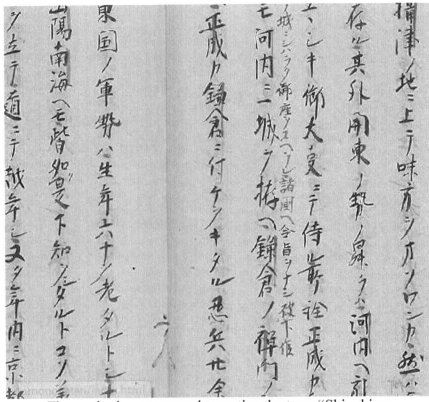

The reader is encouraged to notice the term "Shinobi no Tsuwamono" as contained within this document. This term was not used in the 1300s. The usage of the term "shinobi" began to work its way into Kusunoki Ryu during the 1400s..

This is an excerpt from the Imagawa texts of the *Taiheiki Hidensho*.

The following image comes from the Kusunoki Kaden
(Transmission of the House of Kusunoki):

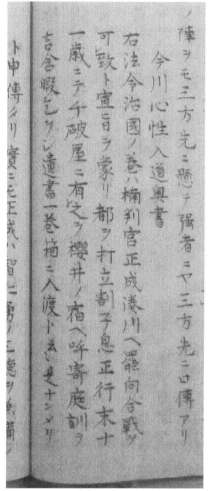

The post script of Imagawa Shinsei Nyodo's chapters of the Kaden

Masashige's Texts

Kusunoki Masashige wrote some of the manuals of the Kaden. However, he signed with a particular name that related to his social standing, containing his court rank and names related to his place in the House of Kusunoki. In a shrine near his home town, he would often sign documents using this preferred name. It is this name that he signs his Kaden text with. Interestingly enough, the presence of Masashige's material in the Kaden shows that Masashige wrote more than the Ikkansho, which many historians consider to be the only document he wrote.

Kusunoki Masashige's preferred signature
(Composed of rank, title, and genealogical names)

Contained within Masashige's sections of the Kaden are the more esoteric ideas, ranging from Buddhist visualizations and Seed Syllables to supernatural powers and discourse on Virtues.

Excerpts of Masashige's passages:

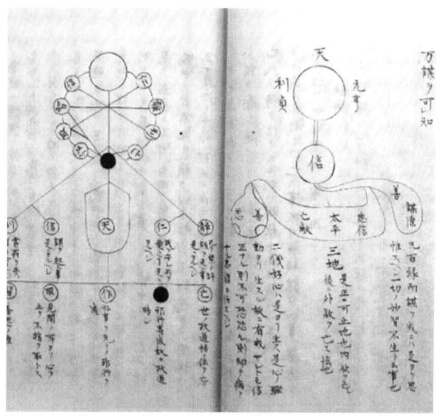

The above diagrams show a foundational teaching for the world view of Kusunoki Ryu. I have provided some rough translation for the key points. I would advise the reader that these two diagrams require an extensive amount of commentary and instructions. Since this is only a brief survey, such detail is beyond the scope of this book

Three Worlds

Great Peace -The true world never ceases (Buddha Field).
Loyalty and Faith -The internal world's enemies are defeated (the world of one's own mind)
Dead Enemy -The external enemies are defeated (the outside projected world).

The Ten Spheres

The Ten Spheres is a teaching that is to be taken on two levels, with different implications for each level. The first level is "internal" and the second level is "government". The Ten Spheres represent either the cycle of changes that a government must go through to survive (repeat the circle) or die (ceases to exists). The other level is concerned with one's internal qualities of leadership (one's own rise and fall). Each sphere represents a stage or quality. If the government is to die off, the Sphere is a stage. If the government is to survive, it is a quality. Here are the Ten Spheres (**with some paraphrasing for clarity**).

Heaven – Ruler Sphere. The sphere serves as the unification of the other nine spheres.
Subdue – Rewards and punishments are done properly.
Faith – Have Faith in your Strategies and Conspiracies
Compassion – To the people, have peace. To your army, have love.
Quiet - Celebrate festivals and allow the people's minds to calm.
Wisdom – Distinguishing virtue from evil
Taking/Choice – Information Gathering prevents your mind from hitting obstacles and prevents hesitation.
Activity – Good is placed first, but wickedness will arise
Darkness- Wickedness manifests. (Here-in resides the potential for government to lose its way)
Death – Eventually, the government's ability to provide peace dies, and changes must be instituted. Government/Leaders must always be willing to die and be reborn. That is, they must be willing to let their approach and policies change and adapt. If they do not, then they will truly die.

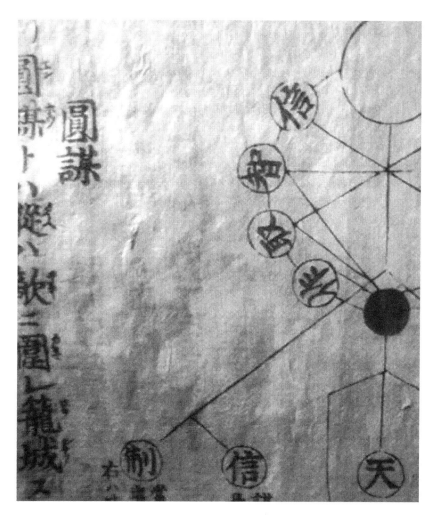

Here is a close-up of the diagram from my own personal copy,
showing slightly different positioning of the connecting lines.

二相大悟
GREAT LIBERATION IN TWO PHASES

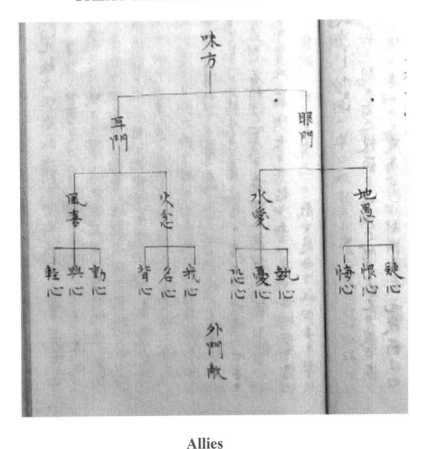

Allies

Gate of the Ear　　　　　　Gate of the Eyes

Wind – Joy　Fire – Anger　Water- Love　Earth –Stupid

Trifle Heart　　　Defiant Heart　　Fearful Heart　Regretful Heart
Pleasure Heart　Prideful Heart　Tender Heart　Resentful Heart
Changing Heart　Selfish Heart　Attached Heart　Distrustful Heart

Outer Gate
Enemy

"Gate of the Eyes" and "Gate of the Ears" goes back to a belief that our perception of the world goes primarily through our eyes and our ears. That is, we interact with our world primarily through our sense of sight and sound. While we possess smell, taste, and touch, we human beings resonate deepest with our eyes and ears.

As such, the teachings of 二相大悟 (Great Liberation in Two Phases) present a view that the Gate of the Ear houses Wind and Fire. This system teaches that Wind manifest as Joy and Fire as Anger. Thus, the Ear houses Wind (Joy) and Fire (Anger).

The Gate of the Eyes contains Water (Love) and Earth (Stupidity).

From each element housed within the Two Gates, three variations of that heart arises, each slightly different.

For example, Wind-Joy gives rise to a Trifling Heart, a Pleasure seeking heart, and an Unstable/Changing Heart.

Water-Love gives rise to a Fearful Heart, a Tender Heart, and an Attached Heart.

While each Element can give rise to the three hearts for its category, there is also a sequence of the arising. For example, a Trifling Heart can give rise to a Pleasure Seeking Heart, which can give rise to an Unstable Heart. Also, under a different circumstance, that sequence can arise in the opposite order, with an Unstable Heart giving rise to a Pleasure Seeking Heart, etc.

In short, this system is a form of psychology, based on the movement of the elements within the hearts of human beings.

As you can see, the word "Ally" appears at the top of the chart, with "Enemy" appearing on the bottom of the chart. The basic meaning of this is that an Enemy can become an Ally through the manipulation of the elements (manipulation of their Eyes and Ears). Consequently, an Ally can become an Enemy through the same process.

That is, those that start as Allies will become enemies if, for example, their Trifling Heart becomes an Unstable Heart. If their Fearful Heart becomes an Attached Heart, they can turn as well.

As such, it is Masashige's instruction to also manage the psychological make-up of your allies, as well as yourself. That is, psychology was a crucial aspect of Kusunoki Ryu.

Another way of viewing this is that a Kusunoki Ryu trained operative must keep a constant management over the psychological health and the psychological health of their allies. This same management of the psychology could also be used against enemies to turn them into allies. This could mean that you gain their trust or you cause them to fight other enemies (getting them to unwittingly do your work for you).

For example, if an ally's wind element is suffering, it must be attended to and balanced. If left unchecked, the ally will develop a Trifling and Unstable Heart, which will cause them to become an enemy.

Furthermore, one has to manage one's own Ears and Eyes, because one's own mental fermentations can bring one to ruin.

It should also be noted that the kanji "heart" can also be read as "mind". In that case, the reader should be aware that "Unstable Heart" can be read "Unstable Mind". Of course, the meaning is the same.

This teaching also goes hand in hand with such teachings as 'Mushin" or "No Mind". Rather than having a consciousness filled with these various "hearts/minds" (the elements in various level of disarray) one should seek Mushin 'No heart/No Mind". As was explained in the Fukushima Ryu commentary, when there is a stop to the various elemental movements (the numerous fetters labeled "mind") then the consciousness experiences relaxation. Within that relaxation, wisdom and clarity arise. This is where the mind of Faith and the mind of Compassion arise.

This teaching is mentioned in the Hijutsu manuals as well.

Mind of Faith and the Mind of Compassion

The mind of Faith and the mind of Compassion are considered to be manifestations of wisdom, not mundane in nature. As such, such qualities do no arise in the mundane way that the above mentioned hearts/minds arise (through normal psychology). Qualities such as Compassion and Faith are deliberately trained and expressed by a focused mind, and are outside the realm of 'Eyes and Ears".

Esoteric Buddhism and Spells

The main Kusunoki Ryu is filled with esoteric Buddhism and spells. Originally, the magic found in Kusunoki Ryu was predominantly Buddhist. As generations passed, several Taoist and Shinto spells were absorbed into the different traditions (such as the spells in Fukushima Ryu and Natori Ryu, etc.)

Seed Syllables used for Esoteric purposes

Kusunoki Ryu is based on the Esoteric Buddhist worldview. Kusunoki Ryu teaches that the world is a magical display of the Buddha Fields. All phenomena are rooted in the five elements. The five elements are displays of the five primordial wisdoms. All happiness is the result of being closely connected to the primordial wisdom and all suffering is being disconnected from the primordial wisdom.

Kusunoki Ryu, and all the descended traditions, contain a considerable amount of magic. However, there is a distinction between the "magic" born from primordial wisdom (Buddhist ritual) and the "worldly magic" that relies on worldly gods and spirits (as discussed in the Fukushima Ryu commentary).

For primordial powers, Masashige teaches the utilization of mantra, mudra, and invocation of syllables. Masashige also presents some useful visualization/chants. The following are two exampes:

- When needing to move about covertly among the enemy, especially when trying to make a covert escape, one should visualize the gods bowing to Avalokiteshvara and chant the name of the Lord of Compassion. An alternate version instructs to visualize Vishnu, after his conversion to Buddhism, and chanting Avalokiteshvara's name.
- When you wish to influence someone to your will, you should visualize Amaterasu radiating light and chant her name.
- When needing protection, visualize Hachiman Daibosatsu and chant his name. You can also do this with Fudo Myo O.

Supernatural Powers

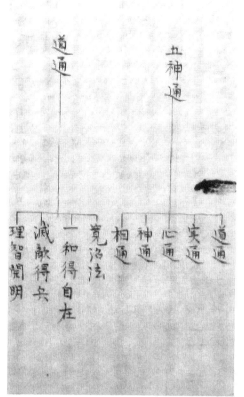

Categorization of Spiritual Powers

Masashige laid out a system of supernatural powers, based on the 5 Divine Powers as taught in Buddhism. These powers are not based on primordial wisdom, but rather, karmic results. This is the difference between "primordial wisdom" and "worldly magic".

Seeing ghost/demons, reading minds, seeing the future, cutting deals with gods, etc. all can be done by unliberated minds if the proper rituals are undergone. However, as Nojiri Narimasa warned in the Fukushima Ryu manual, these rituals can bring one to ruin if their mind is not properly trained prior to diving into sorcerer.

Kusunoki Ikkansho

The original Kusunoki Ikkansho was written by Kusunoki Masashige and presented to his sons (mainly his eldest son, Kusunoki Masatsura) shortly before his death in 1336. It was a single scroll containing the essence of each technique. There currently exists a historical document by this name, however, it is highly debated if this Ikkansho is the original manual. Some scholars believe it to be a pure fabrication, some believe it to be the original, and the remaining scholars believe it to be a recreation based on the original. I believe it to be a recreation based on the original.

Why? It goes back to Imagawa Nyodo. The existence of the word "Shinobi no Tsuwamono" in the Ikkansho suggests that the known copy of the Ikkansho is probably a recreation of the original. Also probable is that, when the original was transcribed in the 1400s, original terms were updated with the terminology of the time.

In the known root texts of Kusunoki Ryu, "shinobi" are referred to by other names (to be addressed later in the survery). Thus, it appears rational to assume the current Ikkansho document is a transcription, or a recreation, written in the later 1400s.

Kusunoki Ryu Kuden Hisho

This book is, essentially, a more elaborate version of part of the Onchi no Maki pieced together with other pieces of various manuals. It serves to deliver commentary on the various other texts, and as such, will not be discussed in detail during the course of this work.

Dozens of Heiho Manuals

There are dozens of warfare and tactics manuals within the Taiheiki Hiden. One of the most extensive is known as "Kusunoki's Military Classic". The title of this text can, ironically, be read as "Kusunoki Ryu's War Sutra". This text will not be addressed in this survey, but the reader should know it contains a vast catalogue of the military tactics of the system.

Shoninki (and the various Dakko no Maki)

While not part of the standard lineage of Kusunoki Ryu, it is a key document of the Natori Ryu. As is known by many of the readers now, Natori Ryu was also known as Shin-Kusunoki Ryu. It was an offshoot of the lineage of Kusunoki Fuden. The story behind this is that the lord of the Kishu province was an avid student of Yui Shosetsu, who was the inheritor of Kusunoki Fuden's lineage. Yui Shosetsu, however, was executed as a criminal during the Keian Rebellion (an uprising of ronin). Yui Shosetsu was the leader of the rebellion, and because of this, many of the people close and related to him were either punished or executed. These executions effectively terminated the direct succession of Kusunoki Fuden's lineage. While many top students remained, the actual inheritor and his immediate family were all gone. Also to be noted, the Kishu lord was also punished with a house-arrest/imprisonment in Edo that lasted for years.

When he finally returned to Kishu, he wished to see Fuden/Yui's teachings live on. Natori Sensei, head of his own family's system of Natori Ryu (rooted in his grandfather's service to the House of Takeda), was tasked with studying with several of the surviving top students of Kusunoki Fuden's lineage, such as Shimazu Sensei. From men like Shimazu Sensei, Natori Sensei learned this version of Kusunoki Ryu. At this time, the Kishu lord then ordered Natori to change the name of the school to Shin-Kusunoki Ryu. Initially, the school then operated under both names. However, the name "Natori Ryu" eventually won out.

The Natori Ryu's Shoninki and accompanying Dakko-no-Maki (such as the Dakko-no-Maki and the Kusunoki Ryu Ninpo Dakko-no-Maki) are very important documents because they not only contain deep insight to shinobi-no-justu, but they also clearly show the Kusunoki Ryu heritage.

One such connection is the usage of using a unit divided into two parts, the "light group" and the "dark group". In the original Kusunoki Ryu, this technique teaches that half of the commando unit travel with lit torches and the other half travels off to the side without any light (blacked out unit). The unit with the torches serves as bait for ambushes/attackers. When the light unit is attacked, the blacked out unit comes from behind and ambushes the attackers.

This technique was originally designed for units, but was modified for a single shinobi and his assistant. We see this technique appear within the Shoninki, in which a shinobi sends his assistant walking down the road with a lantern. The shinobi travels in the dark. If the assistant is attacked, the shinobi can then ambush the attacker.

This technique can also be used to capture individuals, with the servant holding the lantern distracting the target while the shinobi sneaks up behind the target and apprehends them.

Fukushima Ryu Shinobi-no-Maki

I will not address this manual extensively at this time, as an entire commentary for this manual was provided earlier. At this time, I will only remind the reader that many of the individuals involved in founding the Fukushima Ryu were Southern Court Emperors and Loyalists. The fact that Kumazawa Morihisa, an actual Southern Imperial family member, served as a chief retainer to Fukushima Masanori should leave many readers in shock. Furthermore, the espionage network of the House of Fukushima went through Kumazawa and the House of Nojiri (Remember, House of Nojiri is the same house as the House of Kumazawa). With this manual, we can see a confluence of Southern Court techniques, Kusunoki Ryu techniques, and Genji techniques.

This ends the brief overview of selected documents related to the origin of espionage within the system. We will now survey a few select points, taken from the *Kusunoki Kaden* and the *Onchi-no-Maki*.

Selected teaching from

軍用秘術

Gunyo Hijutsu
"Secret Arts Utilized During War"
(The final text of the Kusunoki Kaden)

In the beginning, the Southern Court and Kusunoki Ryu did not refer to espionage as ninjutsu. Espionage was called "Hijutsu", that is, "secret arts". Thus, it is Hijutsu that evolved into Ninjutsu.

When we examine the Onchi-no-Maki, we will also examine early words for samurai spies found within the Southern Court and Kusunoki Ryu.

For the moment, let us look at a few teachings from the Hijutsu manual.

The text states:

> *"Question: What is a crucial component of War?*
> *Answer: For war, you must have these two:*
> *1.)Jingi**
> *2.) Conspiracy, which is not standard military tactics and involves deception.*
>
> *These two ways are crucial points which a warrior must have. Without them, there is no victory."*

***Jingi** = Composed of the kanji for Compassion and Virtue. However, when used as a compound word, it produces a word which means something roughly like **"Duty"** and **"The moral code of a particular group"**.

*"**Question:** Why is it important to learn names and ranks of the enemy?*
Answer: In normal warfare, one seeks to kill the enemies you see in battle. With Hijutsu, you seek to destroy your enemy through conspiracy. That is, you attack your enemy through vacant openings. As such, you must learn which enemy officers are in charge and their role. This provides you an overview of the framework of the enemy forces. You will specifically target these men, not simply to kill them in combat, but to either manipulate them or to set them up as part of a plot. You will attack their minds/hearts. Therefore, you must know your targets deeply. The first part of this is learning the ranks and names of the officers. A few points to always remember are:*

- *If the enemy general is well respected by officers of decent moral character, this makes it much more difficult.*

- *Inserting many beautiful and normal women into the enemy will disrupt them. Female agents can enter this way, but even male agents will be able to enter easier with the additional female presence.*

- *Forts that allow many women to be present inside are forts that are easy to defeat.*

- *Enemies that are on top of mountains, above you, are difficult to defeat.*

- *If the enemy's geography is standard, it will be easy.*

- *Dye your voice with the colors of love and friendliness and become a fond person. You can attack easily this way.*

- *Securing betrayals is a key component.*

- *Become skilled at arranging clandestine meetings with enemies who you are manipulating. Always keep these meeting secret from everyone not directly involved."*

A brief look at the espionage mentioned in

Onchi no Maki
"The Scroll of Onchi Sakon"

We will now look at the terms for spies as found in the teachings of Onchi Sakon. These terms were replaced by "shinobi" in the 1400s.

The Onchi no Maki says:

"Wickedness is a form of stupidity. Insincerity is a form of wisdom. While these are both morally wrong, they have a use."

With this line, we are then introduced to the following terms for the main types of covert operatives:

-Kansha (Wicked Person) 奸者 (姦者)
-Neisha (Insincere Person) 佞者
- Haka no Mono (Conspirator) 謀ノ者

Kansha means "Wicked Person". In the *Banseshukai,* we see that the word "wicked" has been a name for types of espionage agents since olden times in China. Beyond that, if we look into the *Six Secret Teachings,* we find mention of Wicked Spies and Insincere Spies. However, this is a subtle mention and has been missed by many of the English translations. One needs to look at the actual Chinese to see these agents mentioned. The reason for this is that the agents are often not referred to by the name "Wicked Person", but merely the name "Wickedness". Thus, many translators mistake the kanji for referring to a quality and not an actual type of agent.

These two types of agents are listed in the segment called "The King's Wings" when the Yushi (playful/wandering officer) is mentioned. The primary function of the Yushi is listed as *"Find out the enemy's wicked and insincere".* This **does not mean** "the enemy's qualities of wickedness and insincerity". The line is best translated as *"The yushi reveals the enemy's wicked spies and insincere spies."*

"Neisha" is named after the ability of a person to use clever speech and construct realities that are false. While this is a form of high intelligence, it is still considered immoral because it involves falsehood. However, during times of war and extreme need, it can become skillful means.

Haka no Mono is a strategist-spy, a man of conspiracy.

The text states:

"It is good for the Haka-no-mono to also be a Neisha, but not a Kansha."

and

"Many upstanding and brave Haka-no-Mono are Neisha, very few are Kansha. In general, outside of warfare and extreme situations, you should work to suppress all wickedness and insincerity."

and

"Neisha start off as allies, but eventually turn into enemies. For this reason, insincerity has a place and time, and should not be kept around beyond its use.

Enemies will always try to suppress the use of your Haka-no-Mono, and so you have to employ them in conjunction with their role as Neisha."

That means that, because of the horrific reality of warfare, a Haka-no-Mono should be viturous and of utmost moral fiber. They should become neisha during times of great need (i.e. war) because it is a skillful role. However, they should not maintain that level of insincerity outside of warfare.

In a better world, a Haka no Mono could operate without any questions of moral conduct being breached.

However, in such a world, warfare would not occur.

But, due to the reality of suffering and the influence of asuras, warfare exists within this world.

Due to this reality, the Haka-no-Mono must engage in "Nei" (insincerity). This is normally morally wrong, but within the context, it becomes a skillful means.

The Onchi no Maki warns that wickedness, and thus functioning as a "kansha", should be avoided. It is not required for Haka-no-Mono to adopt wickedness. The manual also warns that wickedness is often paired with insincerity. That pairing should be suppressed and prohibited. That is, there should be a clear difference between those covert warriors who are neisha and those who are kansha.

So, how does this manifest?

The spy that your lord sends to run a covert operation behind enemy lines is the Haka-no-Mono serving as a Neisha.

"Kansha" refers to Internal Spies, Local Spies, Doomed Spies and Turned Spies. That is, men who are wicked and will turn on their own side. One should take advantage of these men, but never trust them. A sage ruler should never trust the fate of his kingdom with such spies. These spies should not be entertained any longer than needed. Just as they betrayed their lord, they will eventually betray you.

FURTHER SAMPLES OF TEACHINGS

Regarding Torches

The use of torches in the Kusunoki Ryu is not merely a matter of illuminating the terrain for the user of the torch (i.e. using a torch to see), but rather, the majority of teachings regard torches as a tactical tool.

Mentioned earlier, one technique presented in the Kusunoki Kaden involves sending half of your forces (or your allies force, if you have an ally with you) on the main path. As they move at night, they carry torches and create a field of light around them. This group is bait and will be attacked by the enemy. Consequently, the light from the torches also is intended to ruin the night vision of the enemy. Your allies proceed with their torches through the enemy's territory while your guerilla force moves through the darkness. This technique causes the enemy to focus on the allies and miss the actual guerilla force. This allows for evasion and/or surprise attacks by the guerilla forces moving in the darkness.

Torches were also used extensively as ambush tools and "area-denial tools". It is common in Kusunoki Ryu to set fire to an area for the purpose of ambushing soldier. The various roots texts contain numerous passages explaining how to factor time and weather into setting various types of terrain on fire. The most common techniques involve lighting grasslands on fire so that the wind will drive the fire toward the enemy. This also serves the purpose of buying time for guerilla forces to escape a location.

In a technique named "Fire of the Bird Taking Flight", scouts are sent forth through the wilderness and, using special torches to signal each other, lead the guerilla force through the wilderness. This is said to prevent the enemy from seeing and feeling the guerilla force's presence in the enemy's territory.

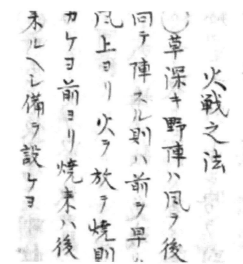

"The Methodology of Incendiary Warfare"
From the *Kusunoki Kaden*

When the fire is meant diminish the number of enemy soldiers, the fire is primarily used as an ambush weapon. Fire is also used to keep the enemy from entering or crossing a particular location, becoming a form of "area denial". As stated previously, this was usually for the purpose of either allowing a guerilla force to escape or to buy time while a larger force shows up to reinforce the smaller guerilla unit.

Adaptation to Terrain

"When there is a mountain, use the mountain in the strategy. When there is fire, use fire in the strategy. When there is water, use water in the strategy. When there is a forest, use the forest as part of the strategy."

-Kusunoki Kaden

Escape From Certain Death

Of all the battle methods found in Kusunoki Ryu, this single method is one of the hallmark formations. It is found in all the various branches and permutations of Kusunoki Ryu. This techinque stems from an idea presented in the *Six Secret Teachings.*

Not a specific formula, it is more of an ideology. The fundamental principle is to always have your forces split into complementary forces, to have spies and commandoes behind enemy lines, and to rely on fire and water. In this methodology, the fire is used for area denial and to buy time. Water is used for a last ditch escape. In this methodology, the guerilla force should always have an escape route that leads to a body of water (lake, rivers, etc) in which they have boats ready for escape. In a variation of this technique, the boats are used to make temporary pontoon bridges. Once the guerilla fighters and crossed the water, the boats are quickly dispersed, leaving the enemy unable to pursue the guerilla force. Naturally, this type of warfare requires excellent timing and communication between units.

Crow Cloud Formation

This formation also comes directly from the *Six Secret Teachings* and is a hallmark of Kusunoki Ryu. This formation is unique in that it is not an actual formation. Unlike typical formations which have the soldiers positions in organized lines and units, this formation calls for free-flowing of the army.

That is, the two units free roam the terrain, supporting the other unit as needed. The idea is that the two units are two murders of crows (crow cloud), freely fluxing across the sky.

Battle Formations

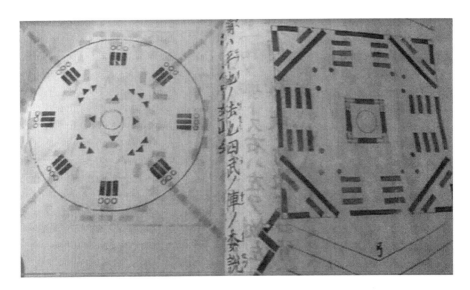

As with all warrior traditions that formed in old Japan, the Kusunoki Ryu contains a handful of battle formations. The battle formations of the system originate in the battle formations of older Chinese methods.

Kusunoki Ryu contains a very esoteric and spiritually moving "origin story" for the esoteric nature of battle formations. Essentially, Kusunoki Ryu views the battle formations as manifestations of the primordial elements and their dynamics.

"From the original state, there arose a single principle. That principle gave rise to the 10,000 things. Foremost, there arose the five directions and five elements. These began to move, and gave rise to In and Yo. From these, the Eight Trigrams arose. From the movement of these Eight, the Sixty Four Hexagrams arose."

The following pictures are presented, in the *Kusunoki Kaden*, as the root diagrams and the fundamental battle formations.

This diagram is based on the Later Heaven Arrangement.

The commander is always "Center/Space" and the remaining four warriors (out of a unit of 5) embodied a particular direction and element, etc.

In this diagram, the four cardinal directions are the "Yo" (Yang) Warriors and the remaining four intermediate directions are the "In" (Yin) Concealed Units. The kanji for the concealed unit is "奇", which means "*unconventional*".

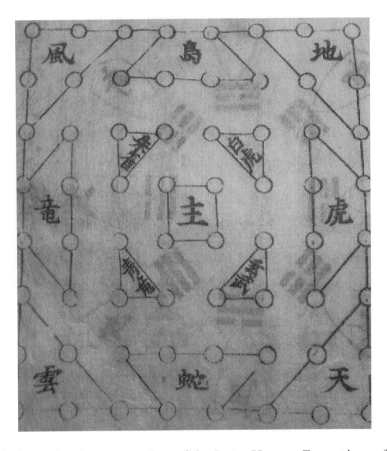

This formation is an extension of the Later Heaven Formation, often times refered to as the "Eight Trigram Formation".

The King's Wings

The Kusunoki Kaden also presents the "King's Wings" teaching from the *Six Secret Teachings*. However, rather than mentioning "Roving Officer" as its own category, the Kusunoki version blends the Roving Officer's role into the role of the Tactician. It is within that grouping that the "Haka-no-Mono" is placed, presumably taking the place of "Roving Officer" (fulfilling the same role.)

The Importance of "Faith"

The importance of "faith" in Kusunoki Ryu is paramount. The esoteric teachings of Kusunoki Ryu provide that faith is the origin of the wonderous arts. Faith is the origin of tactics and skillful means. Without Faith, one cannot arrive at victory and one cannot arrive and truth.

If the reader thinks back to the final scroll of the Fukushima Ryu, they will remember Nojiri's words:

"One follows intuition, with faith, and reaches the truth."

There is the primordial truth. From this truth, light radiates into the darkness. The darkness is your ignorance and the light rays are the *"established paths"* to return to the primordial truth. These light rays are "faith" and riding these light rays back to the truth is "intuition".

Even the *Bansenshukai* teaches that Faith is the foundational quality, the (earth) element in which all the other elements are set.

Shinobi-no-mono for covert scouting

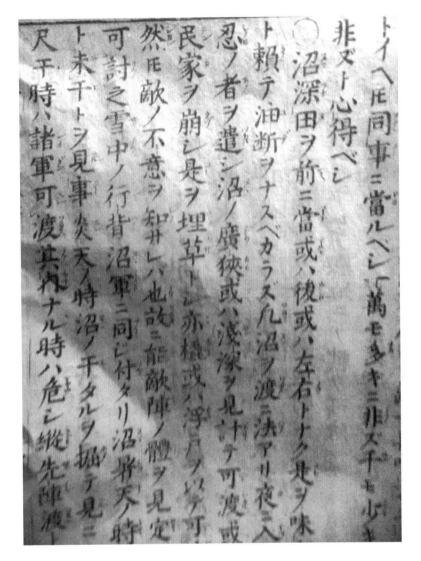

I wanted to add this page from Kusunoki Masatora's manual. On this page, we see an entry discussing the deployment of shinobi. In this entry, the shinobi is deployed to survey the landscape of marshlands at night. We also see the use of special footwear and floatation devices. I also have put this entry in this survey to evidence that Masatora does in fact use the term "shinobi-no-mono".

All Under Heaven

I have chosen to end this brief survey with a quote taken from the Kusunoki Kaden. This quote is taken, word for word, from the *Six Secret Teachings*.

"**King Wen asked**: *How do we establish measures so that we have the allegiance of all under Heaven?*"

T'ai Kung replied: *All Under Heaven is not the domain of a single man. All Under Heaven means exactly what is says—**All Under Heaven**. Those who share profit with all the people under Heaven will gain the entire world. One who withholds the profit for himself will lose the world. Heaven has its seasons, Earth has its resources. Sharing such things in common with the population is authentic humanity. Wherever there is authentic humanity, All Under Heaven will give their allegiance. Sparing the population from death, reducing the hardships of the people, easing their misfortunes, and maintaining even the extremities of the people (handling minority group concerns) is virtue. When there is virtue, All Under Heaven give their allegiance. Sharing the concerns, happiness, likes and dislikes of the people is the righteous way. People will naturally follow such righteousness.*"

This principle of Kusunoki Ryu is also a key principle of the Southern Court Loyalists, as it was a key aspect to the ideology of Go-Daigo and his intended government.

Even in the modern day, the Southern Court Loyalists continue to maintain this ideology that the leader is a function of the people. Even Kumazawa Hiromichi, in the 1950s, often said *"We will let the People decide this issue"*.

Chapter 5

Conclusion

Espionage and Magic: Two Distinct Aspects

Now that this commentary is concluded, I would like to return to a point that I have attempted to make clear numerous times throughout this book. The material presented in the Fukushima Ryu Shinobi-no-Maki represents only a small portion of the entire system. The manual only addressed select magical rites, tools, and techniques (items that, according to the Annotations, were selected by Fukushima Masanori himself). The espionage techniques of the House of Nojiri did not make an appearance in the manual beyond allusions and minor references. This needs to be clear in the mind of the reader.

The origins of the spells presented in the manual may have various origins, some of which may or may not run parallel to the tradition of espionage. As I have presented, numerous times through this work, the espionage originates with Southern Court Loyalists and associated systems, such as Kusunoki Ryu. However, the magic comes from a variety of sources, some material possibly coming from other shinobi traditions. While the majority of spells, by all analysis, appear to come from Owari and Ise, a full knowledge of the origins and the routes of transmission of the various spells does not exist in the oral history nor the historical record.

With that said, I am compelled to make a single point extremely clear: The distinction between the origins of the various spells and the origin of the espionage tactics does not negate either. In other words, even if the spells have an origin in another shinobi system and/or sources outside of Ise and Owari (as unlikely as that may be), the fact that the espionage stems from the Southern Court Loyalists does not change. The oral traditions and the historical records all evidence and agree on this point. Thus, there is no conflict between the two aspects.

Thus, I encourage the reader to keep these two aspects (the magic and espionage) separate in their mind. This also reflects the view of Nojiri Narimasa when he says that magic comes after the shinobi arts are well seasoned in the mind of the practitioner. Interestingly enough, after the formation of the Fukushima Ryu, the issue of different origins (between the magic and the espionage) becomes nullified. That is, after the formation of Fukushima Ryu, within the context of the historical record and within the context of the Fukushima Ryu itself, the two steams of tradition merge into a single tradition.

For those who may, for various reasons, feel compelled to press this issue, I would like to state all examination of the magic points to an origin in Owari and Ise. To be fair though, it is true that the House of Nojiri had property in Omihachiman during this time period. Many Nojiri used this property as a safe house during the end of the Sengoku and the early Edo period. It is plausible and possible that some of the magic may have come from this region. However, even if this is true, it may be equally plausible that the magic was imported from Ise and Owari to Omihachiman. Again, the magic bears all the marks of Owari and Ise based magic.

Further still, I must mention a possible origin for some of the material, which is as both intriguing as it is difficult to research. The Southern Court capital of Yoshino was steeped in Buddhism, Taoism and Shugendo. This is well established. However, among the Buddhist canon in Japan, there exists a section of non-Buddhist texts. These texts contain material from India (Hindu) and the Middle East (i.e. Persian religions, Zoroastrianism, etc) which traveled the Silk Road to end up in China and Japan. Naturally, the Southern Court's collection of religious document is Taoist, Buddhist, Shinto, and Shugendo. However, a small portion of the material is related to India (Hindu) and the Middle East.

In researching this material, I have found that a portion of shinobi magic (from various schools) appears to have some origin in various spells used in India. Some of the spells from various shinobi traditions are almost exact matches of spells from Indian spy manuals, and some of the diagrams of various philosophical and tactical techniques appear to be teachings from the Middle East that were adapted and reorganized to run within a Buddhist/Shinto worldview.

Further work needs to be done by historians and interested parties on this material.

With all this said though, again I must state, that after Fukushima Ryu is established, the magic and the espionage is matched into a single tradition. After the early 1600s, one can simply point to Fukushima Ryu as the origin of the material.

It is the opinion of the author that the magic originated in the Ise and Owari region, with some spells having a possible heritage stemming from Yoshino. It is also my opinion that the House of Nojiri possessed this magic long before the Fukushima Ryu was constructed.

Follow-up: The House of Fukushima

The Tokugawa Shogunate was always very distrusting of the House of Fukushima. The House of Fukushima had been very stable and staunch supporters of the House of Toyotomi. After Toyotomi's death, the House of Fukushima seemed to only side with the Tokugawa at Sekigahara because of Fukushima Masanori's intense dislike and distrust of Ishida Mitsunari.

During the Siege of Osaka (1614-1615), Fukushima Masanori was detained in Edo and not allowed to go near Osaka Castle. This was because the Shogunate believed he would support the last remnants of the House of Toyotomi in the fight. There may have been some truth to this, as Nojiri records show that some Nojiri were sent and did assist the Toyotomi remnants during the Siege. This assistance was not enough and the House of Toyotomi finally disappeared.

Even after this, the new shogun, Tokugawa Hidetada, still did not trust Fukushima Masanori. Convinced that Fukushima would try something, Hidetada became resolved to weaken the House of Fukushima. In 1619, Hidetada cited Fukushima Masanori on a trumped up charge. With that trumped up charge, Hidetada siezed the Hiroshima domain from the House of Fukushima and transferred the House of Fukushima to a small domain in Shinano, present day Nagano Prefecture.

This transfer left the House of Fukushima in financial ruin and the House of Fukushima was forced to let go the majority of their retainers.

However, the House of Fukushima managed to survive into the Meiji Restoration. One such member was Fukushima Yasumasa (b.1852) who served as a general in the Imperial Army. He was known for his horsemanship, his poetry, and for traveling the world. He allegedly participated in some intelligence gathering operations in Siberia and Manchura in the early 1900s.

Follow-up: The House of Nojiri/Kumazawa

Kumazawa Morihisa stuck with Fukushima Masanori through the transition from Hiroshima to Shinano. He remained a loyal chief retainer until Masanori passed away in 1624. After this, Morihisa found service in the Mito Doman, under a branch of the House of Matsudaira. A few Kumazawa and Nojiri continued to serve the House of Fukushima for a few generations after Masanori's death. However, those families eventually made their way back to Owari and Western Honshu. Those Kumazawa and Nojiri that did not stay with the House of Fukushima settled into service with various daimyo in Western Honshu, Kyushu, and Shikoku. Some served as actual retainers, while many served as ronin. One branch became well established within the House of Nakagawa, while other branches (like the aforementioned branches) floated back and forth between Owari and the western provinces.

Eventually, these branches settled in Owari, Osaka, and some settled in the Tokushima Province. The group that settled in Tokushima entered into service with the House of Hachisuka (an old Toyotomi-loyal family that was aligned with the House of Fukushima). A few small groups faded into the landscape of Japan as they settled and became separated from the main lines. So distant are those groups that the main lines, and their branches, do not acknowledge them as relatives anymore.

My own line found itself in Hokkaido after the Meiji Restoration and into the early 1900s. After World War 2, the line left Japan and moved to the United States.

Follow-up: The Southern Court Loyalists

The Southern Court Loyalists, a mentioned previously, continued through the Edo period, through the Meiji Restoration, and continued into the present day. However, at the present time, most of the Loyalists have splintered into various factions. Most of the factions support some member of the House of Kumazawa (as there are currently a handful of Kumazawa individuals who can make legitimate push for the throne), although such activities have decreased in virility in recent decades. When Kumazawa Takanobu withdrew his short campaign (for safety reasons) and died a humble book maker in Osaka, much of the fire behind the House of Kumazawa seemed to leave this world with him. Takanobu Tenno never surrendered or proclaimed himself defeated. He simply could never generate enough force to make a strong enough stand. He always cared and worried for Japan and its welfare. His inability to mount a force strong enough to make significant change, no doubt, haunted him until he died.

After these events, some Loyalists have moved away from the idea of Imperial succession and moved into political activism, utilizing the teachings of the Southern Court and Go-Daigo's ideologies for the purpose of social reform. As a political tool, "Go-Daigo's Intention" makes a powerful grounding for advanced social reform ideologies. These Loyalists have had a fair amount of success in their ventures and instituted several successful reforms and programs in various locations around the world, not just in Japan. In some ways, it seems that "Go-Daigo's Intention" has taken on a life of its own, separate from Imperial restorations.

Still, having said this, there are some Southern Court Loyalists who continue to maintain the full vision of the Southern Court, continue to support Southern Imperial Restoration, and continue to pass this duty and obligation down through their families, generation by generation.

Follow-up: Fukushima Ryu

Fukushima Ryu continued to be passed down within the House of Fukushima for several generations, with Murakami Sensei serving as the last master of the main and official line. However, the system continued to be propagated in Western Japan for several generations as well, spawning several "unofficial" branch lines.

Final Comments

The reader, upon finishing this book, may be tempted to separate the politics of Imperial lines and samurai houses from the magic and the ninjutsu. This attempt may be in effort to better understand the magic and the ninjutsu, with the idea that the politics simply confuses and mires a proper understanding of these two arts.

I disagree and discourage the reader from attempting this approach, and here is the reason:

All of this material is born interdependently. The spirituality and the methodology are not distinguishable from the politics. Think back to the spells. Consider how much of the magic was directly tied to a specific historical person or a specific geographic location. The magic does not invoke some lofty and far removed plane of existence. The magic invokes the very world around the shinobi casting the magic. Power and meaning are not found in invisible worlds located in other dimensions. Power and meaning are found in the very plants, animals, human beings and human events of this present world. This is Shinto. This is the idea that the divine is infused in all of life and all the happenings manifesting around us. Buddhism further explains that all forms are born of the five elements (which are the radiance of the Buddha/Enlightened Mind), all sound is mantra, and all mental movements are a display of the Dharmakaya. The sacred is the very life we are living. We invoke the plants, animals, social events, geographic locations, and specific individuals because we are interdependent with them. We call this interdependent arising "magic", but really, it is just reality structuring and displaying before our perceptions.

With this understanding, hopefully, the reader can see how the politics of the Imperial House and the various houses of samurai are spiritual events. In line with that understanding, I further hope the reader will see how shinobi-no-jutsu is a spiritual thing. Finally, I hope that the reader can see how performing shinobi-no-jutsu in service to one's House, which in turn serves the Emperor, is a form of spirituality.

Conspiracy is a sacred act.

About the Author

Steven Nojiri is a researcher/historian of the samurai and samurai spy culture and history.

First Nations by birth, he married into the Nojiri family early in life and has a keen interest in preserving and protecting Japanese culture and history.

As a First Nations person, he also seeks to preserve and protect First Nations culture and history.

As a Vajrayana Buddhist, he is a dedicated practitioner of the Buddha's Dharma.

Made in the USA
Lexington, KY
29 March 2015